# The Incomparable Cat

# The Incomparable Cat

AMY SHOJAI

FRIEDMAN/FAIRFAX PUBLISHERS

**A FRIEDMAN/FAIRFAX BOOK**

© 1994 by Michael Friedman Publishing Group, Inc.

ISBN 1-56799-064-9

Editor: Karla Olson
Art Direction: Devorah Levinrad
Designer: Edward Noriega
Photography Editor: Anne K. Price

Output by Katz Typographers, Inc.
Color separations by Scantrans Pte. Ltd.
Printed and bound in China by Leefung-Asco Printers Ltd.

For bulk purchases and special sales, please contact:
Friedman/Fairfax Publishers
15 West 26 Street
New York, NY 10010
212/685-6610 FAX 212/685-1307

# DEDICATION

This book is dedicated to the kitties that never find a home; in loving memory.

© Chanan Photography

# ACKNOWLEDGMENTS

Many cat lovers and organizations helped make researching this manuscript a joy, particularly the Sherman Public Library of Sherman, Texas and Karen Elwood. Special thanks to Kathryn Segnar and *Cat Fancy* for thinking of me at the right time; and Dr. Ken Lawrence of the Texoma Veterinary Hospital in Sherman, Texas, who's always been generous with his expertise and time; to Dr. Christopher A. Shaw, Collection Manager, George C. Page Museum, Natural History Museum of Los Angeles County. My deepest appreciation goes to my husband Mahmoud Shojai, who believed in me despite being a confirmed ailurophobe (I'll convert him yet!); to my parents Phil and Mary Monteith, who never doubted I'd succeed; and to Fafnir, my furry muse, who'd meow if he could.

# TABLE OF CONTENTS

The cat is a being like no other. From the cave drawings of prehistoric felines to today's fancy show kitties, cats continue to fascinate people. Though a cat may choose to share its affection with a human or two, it will always retain that quixotic mix of unpredictability and aloof individuality that challenges the understanding of the most patient among us. It is as if they know that when they first stepped into the human ring of firelight, they forever altered our history, influencing our religions, our literature, our art—our very lives.

Whether exalted, as in ancient Egypt, or reviled and persecuted, as during the Middle Ages, the cat has struck an emotional chord deep in the human imagination. It is the envied Wild Brother that cannot be tamed; the Gentle Companion that purrs a mantra to ease aching human souls; the Eternal Kitten that coaxes a smile from the stingiest of human hearts. We delight in our cats—and, we hope, they in us.

Steadfast ailurophiles rejoice that the cat has finally been returned to the pedestal from which it was once so cruelly thrown. Those only recently bitten by the "cat bug" may wonder why it was ever dethroned at all.

Perhaps in today's world, where blind loyalty to one's leaders is no longer expected, where questions are encouraged and individuality is applauded, the cat has finally come into its own. The cat is no longer a god, but neither is it a demon.

This book is for cat lovers everywhere. It is intended as both a basic guide for the neophyte cat addict and a supplement for veteran feline fans. It is my hope that these pages will delight and amuse, surprise and educate, and, most of all, celebrate the mysteries and marvels of all the wonderful cats that share our lives.

Try as we might, it is impossible for us to be indifferent to the cat. But whether we are cat champions or feline foes makes no difference to kitty. Cats are quite satisfied to share their lives with humans by simply being themselves—inimitable cats. And that, dear readers, is more than enough.

## CHAPTER ONE

Whenever a cat takes possession of house and heart, it seems as though it has always been there. In fact, the cat has been around (in one form or another) even longer than people. Ancestors of the modern-day kitty have been found in fossils dating back fifty million years. These archaic predecessors, however, didn't look much like the purring mound of fur that dozes on your lap today.

Taxonomists love to categorize, and the abundant variations of cats found across much of the world give them ample opportunity to do just that. These scientists try to scientifically define the links between different kinds of animals. The first division within the order Carnivora is the family; cats are the family Felidae. Next, groups of animals within the family are divided according to structural similarities; each of these groups is a genus. Finally, animals within a genus are categorized by species, and some even further into subspecies. Because of the many subtle differences among members of the cat family, taxonomists do not always agree on exactly where a specific cat is posi-

The
Evolutionary
Cat

**D**ogs and cats had the same ancestor? I imagine that's a fact that Kitty will try to deny. Just for fun, remind her the next time she swats Fido.

tioned in the family tree; new genera, subgenera, and subspecies are designated as newer variations are identified.

Cats are classified in the order Carnivora (meat-eaters), which had its origin near the dawn of the Cenozoic Era. About sixty-five million years ago, mammals called creodonts evolved with canine teeth for stabbing and sharp-pointed cheek teeth for chewing and shearing meat. The ancestor of creodonts appeared when dinosaurs roamed the earth. When the dinosaurs became extinct, creodonts developed into a variety of predators; some were large, wolf-like creatures, with long bodies, short legs, and clawed feet. Although they were slow-moving relative to cats, creodonts were efficient hunters. In fact, they were able to spread across much of the earth, flourishing for about nine million years. When slow prey were gone, creodonts had to switch to faster newcomer prey for food, the ancestors of the horse and deer. Fossil remains indicate that the creodont brain was quite small. They were so slow both physically and mentally that they couldn't adjust to the faster, much smarter prey, and eventually became extinct.

The earliest probable forebears of today's kitties evolved during the middle Paleocene, about sixty-one million years ago. These forebears were small, insectivorous animals of the family Miacidae, which formed the two branches that gave rise to all of the families within the order Carnivora. Miacids were forest-dwelling creatures that were smaller than their creodont predecessors. However, miacids did improve on brain size and, subsequently, intelligence.

**D**inictis came into existence too late to reach Australia. A nearly parallel, yet separate evolution among marsupials took place, however, giving rise to prehistoric "cat" versions of animals with saber teeth and kangaroo pouches. Fossils have been found in Australia of the Marsupial Lion Thylacoleo, a leopard-size animal with stabbing incisor teeth.

Miacids were enormously successful carnivores; what they lacked in size they made up for in ferocity. The first miacids probably looked like modern-day shrews, with short legs and long bodies. They probably had retractable claws and were at home climbing trees—just like today's house kitties. At the beginning of the Oligocene Epoch, about forty million years ago, a burst of evolution and diversification of the miacids produced all of the modern families of the order Carnivora. These include members of the raccoon family (Procyonidae), the bear family (Ursidae), the dog, fox, jackal, and wolf family (Canidae), the weasel and badger (Mustelidae), the civet, genet, and mongoose family (Viverridae), the hyaena family (Hyaenidae), and of course the entire cat family (Felidae). All of these can be traced back to the pint-sized miacids.

Cat-like carnivores comprise two groups: the paleofelids (family Nimravidae) and the neofelids (family Felidae). Although cat-like in many anatomical features, paleofelids are not direct ancestors to modern cats. (For example, Dinictis was a paleofelid that was nearly the size of a modern-day lynx, with a brain smaller than that of modern-day cats. Its teeth were similar to present-day cats' teeth, too, but with larger canines.) Scientists split the Felidae into two subfamilies: Machairodontinae and Felinae. (Both subfamilies had a common ancestor similar to Pseudaelurus, which lived in the early Miocene to early Pliocene Epochs, about four to twenty-four million years ago.)

Lion

Smilodon

Pseudaelurus

Miacid

Illustrations by Pat Ortega

ale cats are called "Toms," female cats are called "Queens." A cat has a "litter" of kittens, but a group of kittens is known as a "kindle" of kittens. Several cats together can be called a "clowder," "cluster," or "clutter" of cats.

Machairodonts had enlarged saber-like upper canines and began to appear in the early Oligocene Epoch thirty-four million years ago. These cats couldn't use their huge canine teeth unless the mouth was wide open. With the longest upper canines, Smilodon was the latest and most advanced sabertoothed cat. Smilodon's large canines, in conjunction with massive neck and upper body muscles, were used to deliver lethal bites to soft-tissue areas of the neck or belly of large prey. Their prey were probably juvenile mammoths, mastodons, and other thick-skinned mammals. Evidence suggests that Smilodon lived in social groups and could both roar and purr.

The Felinae evolved into cats that were smarter, more adaptable, and swifter hunters than their sabertoothed brethren. One of the earliest was Pseudaelurus, which didn't have huge saber-like teeth, and killed prey by a bite to the neck—like modern cats. Central Europe became home to a variety of lynxes and giant cheetahs; huge tigers evolved in China; North America's forests echoed with the growls of giant jaguars; and an assortment of smaller cats developed and flourished over much of the earth. The fos-

sil bones of Pseudaelurus look very similar to the bones of our smaller modern cats. All existing felines evolved from animals like these.

About three million years ago, Felinae developed into the two distinct genera we recognize today, and they are grouped by size. *Panthera* includes lions, tigers, panthers, and jaguars. In addition, there are two big cats with such unusual differences that scientists have designated specific genera for each: *Acinonyx* for the cheetah, and *Neofelis* for the clouded leopard. *Felis* is the genus of the smaller cats, including the domestic varieties. This means that the kitty sharing your sofa belongs to the family Felidae, genus *Felis,* species *silvestris,* subspecies *catus.* With a title like *Felis silvestris catus,* is it any wonder Kitty carries such an air of importance?

Experts and scientists have argued for years over the direct ancestry of the domestic house cat. The Martelli's wildcat is a probable close relative but not the missing link we seek. Martelli's wildcat inhabited Europe and the Middle East and became extinct relatively recently (about a million years ago). Some scientists consider this animal a probable direct ancestor of our modern small wildcats, *Felis silvestris.* It is these modern wild cousins that are suspect, because they bear such a distinct resemblance to domestic cats.

Wildcats are found in Europe, Asia, Africa, and America and are the same genus as domestic cats. For many years it was held that domestic varieties were direct descendants of the European wildcat or forest cat, *Felis silvestris silvestris.* However, although the European wildcat is superficially similar to domestic cats, the two species are very different. The European wildcat's body is more heavily built, its limbs longer, its skull broader, and its tail shorter and blunt, rather than tapered and pointed on the end like tails of domestic cats. The European wildcat is also nearly impossible to tame. Experts have since concluded that these factors eliminate the probability of its close ancestry with the domestic cat.

Another contender is the Asiatic steppe wildcat, or desert cat, *Felis silvestris ornata*. This cat is smaller than the other wildcats and is found from the Soviet Union south to central India. It is thought by some to figure in the genetic picture, perhaps in conjunction with the African wildcat.

The most likely origin for domestic cats, most experts agree, is the African wildcat, *Felis silvestris lybica*. Its tail is long and tapering like domestic varieties, and although it is slightly larger than house cats, it looks much more similar to them than does the European wildcat. A majority of the mummified remains of Egyptian domesticated cats were of this African variety, which domesticates easily and will readily interbreed with domestic cats.

Cats were most certainly domesticated 3,500-4,500 years ago; we have only to look to ancient Egypt to be convinced of this. However, experts speculate that cats came into homes as partners and pets long before ancient Egyptians began singing their praises, and scientists continue to search for proof.

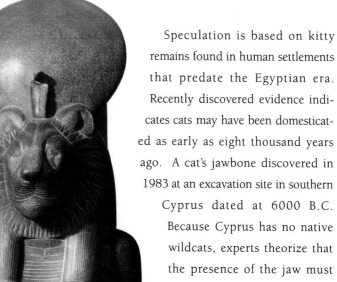

Speculation is based on kitty remains found in human settlements that predate the Egyptian era. Recently discovered evidence indicates cats may have been domesticated as early as eight thousand years ago. A cat's jawbone discovered in 1983 at an excavation site in southern Cyprus dated at 6000 B.C. Because Cyprus has no native wildcats, experts theorize that the presence of the jaw must mean the cat was brought by human settlers. This could mean that cats have been enriching human lives nearly twice as long as previously believed.

In any event, cats have been around a long, long time. Their knowing attitude and aura of eternal agelessness are constant reminders that cats spring from the mystic beginnings of time itself. It's a fact Kitty will never let us forget.

*Early Egyptians celebrated the lion, and later the cat, as symbols of power. This lion-headed goddess is Sekhmet, which means "the powerful." The lion often represented the sun god, Ra. Sekhmet, Tefnet, and Bast were Ra's daughters, and Bast became identified with the domestic cat.*

Right: Panthera leo, *a lioness.*

Far right: Felis silvestris catus, *a domestic cat*

## BIG VS. LITTLE

The cat species vary in weight from four pounds (1.8 kg) to more than six hundred pounds (272.2 kg). Big cats rest with their forelegs straight out in front of them, leave their droppings uncovered, and completely pluck bird prey before eating it. Most small cats (including domestic cats) curl their paws under their chests when at rest, bury their feces, and eat fur, feathers, and flesh, spitting out only the longest feathers of birds they catch.

# Lions and Tigers and...
# Cats, Oh My!

As your kitty calmly washes his whiskers, take a moment to consider: What exactly does that spritely, purring kitten have in common with other cats around the world? How are they alike—and what are their differences?

As mammals, all cats share certain similarities. Cats are warm-blooded, and they give live birth and suckle their young. With subtle differences, most cats of the world are very much alike in behavior. The tabby that stalks and pounces on your ankle mirrors the stealthily stalking leopard that hunts to capture its dinner. The physical family likeness includes feline eyes set well forward in a basically short face; a lithe, muscular, fur-covered body; and certain physiological specializations and behavioral similarities that distinguish cats the world over.

Members of the cat family are so closely related, in fact, that crossbreeding between species is quite possible. Wildcats often mate with domestic cats, and crossbreeding between wildcat species is likely to occur. The "leopon," a cross between a leopard and a lion, and the "tigon," a cross between tiger and lion, are frequently produced in zoos. However, crossbreeding between big-cat species in the wild rarely occurs, and new "breeds" are unlikely, since the hybrid cubs are often sterile. But the fact that such breedings actually take place is testament to the adaptability and similarity of cats around the world.

The cat species vary in weight from four pounds (1.8 kg) to more than six hundred pounds (272.2 kg).

The skeletal structures of all cats are very similar, with only minor variations detectable by specialists. The most obvious distinction between wild and domestic cats is their disparity in size. This difference evolved in part because large animals were the most available prey to wild cats. Zebra and antelope become kitty vittles only when cats are big enough to catch them. Size differences also make it possible for a variety of cat species to live near each other without stepping on each others' furry toes by competing for the same food.

Environment also dictates the distinctive fur coat each cat wears. Domestic cats display a tremendous variety of stripes, dots, spots, and swirls. Although evolution initially played a big role in decking them out, more recent colors are due to human taste and selective breeding, rather than environmental adaptation.

The house cats' wild brothers, however, depend on coloration for more than compliments. The dusty-colored sand cat blends into the dunes and scrub that make up its home; long fur that grows on the soles of its feet protect the pads and helps it navigate loose sand. If the sand cat had the bright stripes of the tiger or the characteristic coloring of the black leopard, it would not be able to sneak up on its prey. Each cat is marked in a specific way to aid in its unique fight for survival.

The land bridge to Australia was gone by the time prehistoric cats were evolving. Although Australia has no indigenous cat species, several animals have been given the name "cat." However, the Tiger Cat, *Dasyurus maculatus*, and the Western and Eastern Native Cats, *D. geoffroii* and *D. viverrinus*, of Australia are actually marsupials.

*Right: Only the male lion has a mane. (See the lioness on page 16)*

*Opposite page: The cougar is the largest species in the genus Felis. Also called Mountain Lion, Puma, Painter, and Panther, it ranges from the southern Yukon to South America, including parts of Nova Scotia, the western United States, and Mexico.*

## LION

No one would mistake the lion for anything else. Yet even though the lion may be ten times larger than your kitty couch potato, their behaviors are strikingly alike. The lion's tawny coat and imposing mane give a unique, regal appearance, but the intrinsic kitten quality lingers just below the surface. Royalty evaporates and is replaced by shades of purring kitten when King Leo washes behind his ears with a huge forepaw or dozes sleepily in the sun.

Lions grow up to ten feet (3 m) long, with the tail adding an extra forty-plus inches (one meter plus). Leo's short fur ranges from light buff to intense orange-brown (and sometimes white), and the back of his ears are marked with "false eyes" of black fur. Only the male has a mane, which can be shaded from yellow to black. The lion's mane is the only physical distinction of sex in the cat family, other than reproductive organs; in all other cat species, males and females look alike.

Lions are the only wild member of the cat family to live in social groups, called prides. The pride hunts as a team by chase and ambush. The female is the bread-winner, often chasing prey into another lion's killing embrace. Lions hunt by either night or day, but they are usually active only about four hours at a stretch and spend most of their time sleeping. (Sound familiar?)

Lions, like all cats, are extremely territorial. Vocalizations including coughs and growls, and impressive roars help establish territory. When a new male lion becomes dominant, he often kills the offspring of the previous male to set up his own hierarchy and to induce the females to go back into estrus, or breeding cycle.

The lion is the only wild cat that has a prolonged breeding cycle. Resulting overpopulation is controlled in a barbaric but effective fashion: the strongest eat first and remain strong; the weakest eat the leavings, consequently suffering low fertility and a high abortion rate, and many die of starvation.

When your kitty tires from playing on the drapes, it will search out a comfortable place to curl up and sleep the day away—just like a lion. Professor David McDonald of the University of Oxford, England, has studied cats since 1978 to see if their legendary solitude is fact or fiction. Can cats adapt to group living? His studies conclude that domestic cats also form communal societies. These kitty "prides" were studied in large populations of unaltered domestic cats in farm settings. They are marked by dominance and hierarchy, territorial disputes, and peaceful co-existence— just like lion prides. Domestic females are a bit more liberated than lionesses, however, and may not deign to mate with the "king." Macho male cats, called toms, fight over territory in kitty prides, but even when they win, they don't always get the girl.

Female cats nurse each other's kittens as a matter of course, as do lions. Invading toms often kill undefended kittens as do their lion counterparts. This behavior is nothing new; it was recorded centuries ago in descriptions of the domesticated cats of ancient Egypt.

## ROAR VS. MEOW

A group of two chains of bones that link the larynx to the skull is quite different between the big cats *(Panthera)* and the small cats *(Felis)*. In larger cats such as the lion, one section of these bones is made of elastic cartilage. A pad of tissue at the vocal chords allows the lion to vocalize a roar, which can carry over a five-mile (8-km) distance. In smaller cats, all the sections are inflexible bone, which can at most produce a scream. But, smaller cats are able to purr continuously, vocalizing on both incoming and outgoing breaths. The cat's purr is produced by muscles surrounding the voice box, not from vibrations of the diaphragm and vocal chords as previously thought.

© Russell Grundke/Unicorn Stock Photos

Cougar

## MAN-EATERS!

Older tigers, lions, and leopards will often opt for easy prey, like domestic cattle, when they are unable to obtain game prey because of lost energy, lost teeth, or injury. In some areas, man-eaters have become a problem. Lions and tigers eat people only when there's nothing better—and almost anything else is better. Leopards, however, will kill anything that moves and frequently develop a taste for human flesh. They have been known to attack entire villages when on the rampage. There are certainly times when the ferocity of a riled house cat rivals the man-eaters of India; in these instances, we can be grateful our cats aren't the right size to attempt it.

of killing. They also have been described as being more devious than lions. Tigers are mainly nocturnal and are generally solitary hunters.

Most domestic cats detest getting their fur wet, and it is a patient kitty indeed that submits to a bath. Of course, there are always exceptions to the rule: the Turkish Van loves the water. Close the door if you don't want this water baby joining your bath.

## LEOPARD

The leopard is an elegant-looking cat. It has a distinctive dark pattern of rosettes formed from spots that are scattered across a field of golden fur. Some leopards are black, called "melanistic"; occasionally, the dark rosette pattern will still show through.

*Siberian Tiger*

Leopards, also called panthers, have proportionally smaller heads than other big cats and aren't as heavy in the body as the lion and tiger. Like the lion, the leopard carries "false eyes"—white spots—on the back of each ear. Leopards grow to over six feet long (2 m), with tail adding another forty-three inches (1 m).

Leopards vocalize in series of grunts, coughs, and grating noises but are usually very quiet. They are strong swimmers, good climbers, and ingenious hunters. Leopards have even been reported to fake seizures to attract the attention of prey, then jump up to eat them.

The house cat's repertoire of starvation wails and moaning threats quickly trains the human owners to "feed me before I DIE!" Such adroit manipulation is as ingenious as anything the leopard has to offer.

## TIGER

The Siberian tiger is the largest of all cats; it can grow to over twelve feet long (3.7 m), including the tail. There is great size disparity between kinds of tigers, but coloration always consists of either striped shadings of orange, black, and white, or rarer black-on-white varieties. Tigers look as though they've been colored with broad bold strokes by a child's crayon.

Aside from their distinctive coats, lions and tigers physically look very much alike. However, their personalities are quite different. Lions avoid the water; tigers enjoy swimming. Tigers are much more agile and aggressive than lions and kill not only for food but for the thrill

© Martin Harvey/The Wildlife Collection

*Cheetahs hunt by sight, coursing (running down) their prey rather than ambushing. They prefer open country for hunting this way.*

# CHEETAH

The cheetah is the only species in the genus *Acinonyx* and is anatomically different from all other Felidae. It is the oddest of all felines, halfway between a dog and a cat.

The cheetah wears dark spots on a light field of gold. It is large but slim and has very long legs with a disproportionately small head. Most members of the cat family have fully retractable front claws, but the adult cheetah's narrow paws and toe structure are more like a dog's than a cat's. The nonretractable claws are blunt and worn down, never razorsharp like other cats'. Because of these anatomical differences, the cheetah has a more difficult time climbing than some of the other cats.

The cheetah can run fast in bursts of speed up to sixty miles (96 km) per hour over short distances, and it is the fastest land mammal. Since ancient times, cheetahs have been domesticated and used as hunters and retrievers in Asia and Egypt. Domesticated cheetahs are said to show faithfulness, obedience, and affection toward their masters.

# JAGUAR

The jaguar is the only *Panthera* indigenous to North America, but it has been exterminated in the United States, Mexico, and much of Central America. It can grow to six feet (2 m) long, with an additional thirty-inch (75-cm) tail. A bristly golden coat is dotted with brown or black spots, or rosettes with dots inside. The coat can also be solid black, like the leopard's. Jaguars climb well, like to swim, and often fish.

Most domestic cats share the jaguar's taste for fish. Many, however, prefer eating their fish straight from a can; they mustn't risk getting a paw wet pulling a fish from the water.

## HUNTING TACTICS

The cat's specialization of eyes, claws, and teeth make it ideal for the stalk and ambush. Most cats are solitary hunters, and many are nocturnal, using concealment and stealth to draw close enough to prey to pull it down after a brief, intense rush. Claws hold the prey for the killing bite to the back of the neck, and strong canine teeth sever the spinal cord in an efficient deathblow.

The cheetah is the only cat to "course" its prey, acting more like a wolf than a cat; it often hunts during the day when it can use its eyes to advantage. The cheetah's *coup de grace* is a bite to the throat, a strangling kill rather than the perhaps more swift and merciful back-of-the-neck, spine-severing death stroke of other cats.

All cats are extraordinary athletes, and in addition to being fast, a house cat can jump, on average, up to five times its own height. Some wildcats, such as the desert lynx, are actually able to catch birds by jumping high into the air and knocking them down with their paws.

*Lynx*

## CLOUDED LEOPARD

The clouded leopard is placed by most authorities in its own genus, *Neofelis nebulosa*. It has unique brown-black markings marbled over a light gold field. It is about the size of a small leopard but has a longer body and shorter legs ending in very broad paws. The clouded leopard also has an extremely long tail, and the head is exceptionally large for its body size. It has the largest canine teeth of any other living cat and in this respect most closely resembles the now extinct saber-toothed cats of antiquity.

The Canadian lynx population fluctuates dramatically. A study made in central Alberta showed a variation in population density of 2.3 lynx per 40 square miles (103.6 km²) during the 1966-67 winter, rising to 10 lynx in the same area 5 years later. It is speculated that lynx prefer snowshoe hares to the exclusion of all other food sources, and starve rather than eat other prey. Sounds just like a finicky cat.

© Gerry Ellis/ The Wildlife Collection

# KITTY FINGERPRINT

Big cats have fur that extends all the way down the nose, while in smaller cats (our pets included), the end of the bridge of the nose is exposed. The ridged pattern of a cat's nose leather is like a fingerprint; each is different. Whisker-spot patterns are also as individual as fingerprints.

## SMALL CATS

The genus *Felis* contains a huge variety of species and subspecies. The following represent only a few that are either very similar to, or very different from, domestic cats.

The flat-headed cat doesn't look very much like a cat at all. It has very short legs, a long body, and a short tail with a slightly flattened head. Like the cheetah, it has claws that aren't fully retractable. This cat is among four species (flat-headed, rusty-spotted, fishing, and leopard cats) considered by scientists to be closest to the ancient common ancestor of the whole cat race.

The rusty-spotted cat is smaller than the domestic cat, and is indigenous to southern Sri Lanka and India. In Sri Lanka, it lives in humid mountainous forest, but in India it is found more often in open, grassy country. Agouti gray fur patterns on his head, back, and tail are marked with rusty red spots, blotches, and lines. The underside of its body is white, with large spots. This kitty is easily tamed if taken from the wild as a tiny kitten—but not much is known about its habits.

The fishing cat has slightly webbed paws, with claws that can't be fully retracted. It likes water and has been observed diving to catch fish. The leopard cat is also a fisher and a swimmer and has thus been able to colonize small islands. The leopard cat is unusual in that the males may help raise the young kittens. (In most cat societies, this task is left to the female.)

The Pallas's cat, or manul, is an unusual-looking feline with almond-shaped eyes set in a short, broad, slightly flattened head. It has a long ruff of fur on the cheeks, large, low-set, widely spaced ears, and a massive body with very stout legs. The Pallas's cat is about the same size as a large domestic cat. It produces a scream that sounds like a cross between a screech owl's cry and a dog's bark, but it isn't able to spit or hiss like domestic cats. Speculation that the Pallas's cat was an ancestor of the Persian and Angora breeds is today considered unlikely.

The lynx is the only existing member of the cat family found in both the Old World and the New World, and it ranges over Scandinavia to Siberia, Kashmir, and Tibet; Alaska and Canada to the northern United States; Spain and Portugal; and it has been reintroduced in Switzerland and eastern Europe. It is a sturdy cat with rear legs that are longer than the front legs, big paws, and a short tail. It has long tufts on its ears and its fur ranges in color from sandy gray to tawny red.

Wildcats have a larger body and a slightly smaller brain than domestic kitties and breed only once yearly. Some scientists have divided the wildcat group into up to twenty-three subspecies. Of these, the African wildcat is considered the most like our own domestic breeds and is probably the "founding father" of the cat that is even now warming itself on your hearth.

Big cats, small cats, cats with long hair, cats with no hair, spotted cats, striped cats, dark cats, bright cats—no matter what the package, it's obvious that the nation of cats has no boundaries; cats are recognized as cats the world over. Domestic kitties have traveled quite a distance from their wild origins—or have they?

# SPECIES LIST

genus *PANTHERA*

    Jaguar, *P. onca*
    Lion, *P. leo*
    Leopard (Panther), *P. pardus*
    Snow Leopard, *P. uncia*
    Tiger, *P. tigris*

genus *NEOFELIS*

    Clouded leopard, *N. nebulosa*

genus *ACINONYX*

    Cheetah, *A. jubatus*

genus *FELIS*

    African golden cat *F. aurata*
    Asian golden, *F. temmincki*
    Bay cat, *F. badia*
    Blackfooted cat, *F. nigripes*
    Bobcat, *F. rufus*
    Caracal, *F. caracal*
    Chinese desert cat, *F. bieti*
    Cougar, *F. concolor*
    Fishing cat, *F. viverrinus*
    Flat-headed cat, *F. planiceps*
    Geoffroy's cat, *F. geoffroyi*
    Iriomote cat, *F. iriomotensis*
    Jaguarundi, *F. yagouarundi*
    Junglecat, *F. chaus*
    Kodkod, *F. guigna*
    Leopard cat, *F. bengalensis*
    Lynx, *F. lynx*
    Marbled cat, *F. marmorata*
    Margay, *F. wiedi*
    Mountain cat, *F. jacobita*
    Ocelot, *F. pardalis*
    Pallas's cat, *F. manul*
    Pampas cat, *F. colocolo*
    Rusty-spotted cat, *F. rubiginosus*
    Sand cat, *F. margarita*
    Serval, *F. serval*
    Tiger cat, *F. tigrinus*
    Wildcat, *F. silvestris*
    (23 subspecies)

*Top:* Panthera pardus, *leopard.* *Bottom:* Felis caracal. *The caracal is sometimes called the Desert or African Lynx. It runs like a cheetah, and can leap 6 feet (2 m) into the air to knock down birds.*

# The Naming of The Cat

There is no real way to tell why our feline friends were named as they are, but there do seem to be three distinct origins: names derived from the sounds the cat makes; names based on the action of the cat; and names associated with ancient cat-linked deities. In fact, words for "cat" are very similar the world over. It's likely these words originated with the very first domesticated kitties and have changed little, if any, over the centuries.

Egyptians named the cat *mau*, which signifies "the seer" (from mau, "to see"), perhaps because they associated it with the all-seeing Eye of Horus. Other historians speculate that mau was inspired by the mewing sound that the cat makes. Along those same lines, China's word for cat is *miu*—awfully close to meow, too.

*Puss* seems a natural derivation of Posht or Pasht, which were names used for Bast, ancient Egypt's cat-headed god. Others speculate that *puss* evolved from the Latin words *pusus* and *pusa*, which mean "little boy" and "little girl", respectively. How many of us today affectionately call our cats by similar terms of endearment? Another whimsy connects the French *le puss* to the Latin *lepus*, which means "hare." This connection is not at all farfetched—"puss" was used in England for both cats and hares well into the eighteenth century.

The Romans called the cat *felis* from the root word *felix*, meaning "a good and auspicious omen" linked to magical divination. Later, they began using *catta*, the same name as the weasel, as both cats and weasels were used as vermin catchers.

Other words may stem from an Aryan root word *ghad*, which means "to grasp or catch." This seems a natural descriptive choice; our cats are expert at seizing prey—or affectionately hugging our necks.

## "CAT" AROUND THE WORLD

Arabic—*kittah*

Armenian—*gatz*

Basque—*catua*

Chinese—*miu*

Cornish—*kath*

Egyptian—*mait* or *mau*

French—*chat*

German—*katze, katti* or *ket*

Greek—*kata* or *catta*

Italian—*gatto*

Latin—*felis* or *cattus*

Old English—*gattus*

Polish—*kot* or *gatto*

Portuguese—*gato*

Russian—*kots* or *koshka*

Spanish—*gato*

Turkish—*kedi*

Welsh—*kath*

# History of the Cat

People have been intrigued by the cat since time immemorial. In prehistoric times, humans and cats not only competed as hunters but probably hunted each other as well. The human race has always admired the hunting prowess of cats. Cave drawings of lions in prehistoric art can't be totally explained but point to probable cult relationships. Cat amulets indicate that feline cults have existed since at least Egypt's sixth dynasty. Even a slate palette used for mixing cosmetics dating to 3100 B.C. was embellished with stylized lions.

Later, anthropomorphizing became quite common, and ancient civilizations began mixing the best attributes of humans and animals to invent magnificent mythic beings. One of the most outstanding examples is the famous Sphinx at Giza, outside Cairo, which represents Chephren with a human face and the body and power of a lion.

The lion, the leopard, and eventually the cat joined the bull as major symbols of power and virility in ancient Egypt. Mesopotamian cultures so glorified the cat that it eventually outshone all other anthropomorphic figures. Even today, cats continue to be the universal symbol of the side of nature that cannot be tamed.

## FELINE BEAUTY

The eyes of the African wildcat are rimmed with a dark lining; during the period around 950 B.C. when cats were considered deities, fine Egyptian ladies often lined their own eyes with cosmetics to resemble these cats' eyes.

Cleopatra's famous beauty was said to be enhanced by her extraordinary resemblance to the cat.

*This bronze cat with a decorative collar is typical of the feline figures associated with the cat cult of Bast; such statues were often presented by worshipers as votive offerings.*

*Bast, considered a goddess of fertility, was usually shown as a cat-headed woman: the domestic cat was perhaps even then known for its sexuality.*

## FELINE SACRIFICE

Surviving mummies examined by X-rays reveal that many cats died at ages of less than eighteen months, half were under four months old, and in many cases their necks had been deliberately broken. Despite laws said to have protected cats in Egypt, some cats were bred specifically to be offerings. Sextus Empericus recorded that in ancient Egypt, where the cat was the symbol of the sun-god, many cats were sacrificed to Horus, the rising sun. In a mystical sense, the deity the cat symbolized died for his people when the cat was immolated.

*Mummification for cats wasn't as involved as it was for humans, but only wealthy owners could afford elaborate treatment. These cats were treated with sodium carbonate and sodium bicarbonate (natron) to preserve and dehydrate the body. Then they were wrapped in a linen sheet, followed by careful bandaging. The outer cover was cloth or papyrus and palm leaves woven into a pattern molded to shape kitty ears and features. The head was sometimes painted with eyes, nose and mouth. Cat mummies were placed in pottery jars, cases, or funerary boxes, often designed in a cat shape.*

## CAT ON A PEDESTAL

While historians continue to argue about and postulate exactly when the cat became domesticated, it remains entirely possible that the cat actually domesticated itself. As humans became cultivators, their precious grain stores drew vermin—which in turn called the cat. It seems quite plausible that wild cats so drawn to villages and homes were tolerated and later encouraged to stay and catch mice. How many of us have had a cat adopt us when it simply appeared one day at the back door and appropriated our home as its own?

The first documents relating to the history of the cat's domestication date from Egypt 1668 B.C. Later paintings of cats found in Theban tombs (about 1450 B.C.) show cats collared and tied to chairs in homes. Cats probably did not share a life of luxury early on, however, but had to earn their keep. Some early paintings seem to indicate that cats may have been used as flushers and retrievers of game.

About 950 B.C., a city of the Nile delta called Bubastis worshiped a cat-headed goddess called Bast, or Pasht. She was the favorite of the sun-god, Ra, and was associated with happiness, pleasure, dancing, and the warmth of the sun.

The cat was much admired by early Egyptians for its mystical qualities. The name "Bast" implies "the tearer" or "the render," exemplified by Bast's nightly battle with the sun's mortal enemy, the Serpent of Darkness. Bast was symbolized by the moon, which was believed to be the sun-god's eye during the night; the pupil of the cat's eye waxes and wanes, just like the moon. Even today, the unexpected, eerie glow reflected from a cat's eyes on a dark night is enough to shiver the soul. It's easy to see why Egyptians believed cats held the light of the sun in their eyes.

Sacred cats were protected by Egyptian law, and their care was an inherited honor passed from father to son. Temple cats were watched by the priests, their every move interpreted as a message from the goddess Bast. Vows or requests were made to Bast by partially shaving the head of a child (the amount shaved depended on the vow or request), weighing the clippings, and presenting the cat guardian with an equal weight in silver. The guardian would then tender his charge with an appropriate amount of fish and the cat's movements would be interpreted by the priest. (The record does not say whether a cat's eating the fish was a good sign or a bad one. A finicky cat might have posed quite a dilemma.)

The occasion of a cat's death was great cause for mourning. Herodotus (born about 484 B.C.) was one of the first anthropologists and the earliest Egyptologist. His observations of the cats of Egypt are some of the best documentations of early cat history to be found. "If a cat dies in a private house by a natural death, all the inmates of the house shave their eyebrows," he wrote. He also recorded that dead cats were often mummified and placed in repositories.

Herodotus believed all cats were interred in Bubastis, but excavations revealed that kitty mummies were buried in a number of places. In 1890, over 300,000 mummies (24 tons!) were found buried at Beni Hassan. Sadly, a wonderful opportunity to study these first domestic kitties was destroyed when most were ground up and used as fertilizer. The archaeologists of the time were apparently not particularly interested in cats.

Egyptians jealously guarded their sacred cats, treating them like beloved children, and none were allowed to leave Egypt. However, as is often the case with such "forbidden fruit," the cat became a very attractive and coveted possession in the eyes of outsiders. Ways were found to smuggle the cat out of the country. Although Egyptians religiously sought out and ransomed back as many stolen cats as they could, inevitably some were lost to Egypt forever.

Northwind Picture Archives

## THE TRAVELING CAT

The domestic cat spread from ancient Egypt to the Orient. Initially, Persians believed it to be a carrier of disease and gave it no welcome. The earliest confirmed Indian reference dates to about 200 B.C., and some historians speculate that cats most likely reached China later than India and traveled to Japan from China.

However, some references to the cat in the Far East actually predate the earliest Indian documentation; Confucius is said to have kept a pet cat in 500 B.C. China. One can only assume that a few isolated cats were introduced to China as oddities, not becoming widespread until much later. Toward the end of the sixth century, the cat was associated with the occult in China, but still held a valued

*In China, the lion and tiger were associated with nobility and good fortune. Oriental mythology is filled with fantastic creatures, like this Chinese sphinx, which shares the attributes of man and beast.*

*Right: The Sphinx at Giza, outside Cairo, Egypt.*

*Opposite page: A slate carving of Sekhmet.*

© Art Resource

The Greek word for ferret, *ailouros,* has now somehow become translated into ailurophile and ailurophobe: an ailurophile is a person who loves cats; an ailurophobe is a person who hates or is afraid of cats.

place as a pet with the nobility. These felines shared not only the master's heart and hearth, but also his table, as the main course! Even today, kittens are sold as a feature of Cantonese cuisine.

Conversely, cats in Japan were much revered, and in A.D. 600 were kept in pagodas to guard precious manuscripts. People of Japan believed that a cat crossing the path constituted good luck. The cat in ancient Japan was considered so precious that during the tenth century, and for several centuries thereafter, Japan restricted cat ownership to members of nobility.

The cat next traveled to Europe. The first stop was Greece, followed by Rome, but kitty was not particularly well known in the ancient Greco-Roman civilizations. However, the few that knew cats cherished them; a woman found entombed in the lava of Pompeii was still holding her pet cat in her arms.

Aesop, a Greek author who died in 546 B.C., wrote several fables in which cats figured prominently. Five hundred years later, Palladius of Rome began recommending cats for protection from vermin. Romans had often kept animals, such as ferrets and even snakes, to keep down rats.

The cat spread from the Mediterranean to the far corners of the Roman Empire and beyond. Kitty was probably not bred and distributed like cattle and other domestic animals but instead distributed itself by traveling with people from place to place.

The cat appears to have been quite rare in northern Europe, even after being introduced there around the tenth century. We probably have the lowly mouse to thank for kitty being where he is today. House mice and rats weren't originally European but were brought back from the Middle East by the Crusaders. Seamen took cats along on ships to control this pest, and consequently the cat spread far and wide.

By the tenth century, domestic cats had arrived in England. They remained quite rare, however, and were highly prized as protectors of grain for they killed the rodents that infested the grain. A mid-tenth century Welsh King named Hywel Dda set laws specifying the value of cats, including stiff fines for anyone who killed an adult cat. The value of a cat, and the fine for killing one, was double if the cat was a rat killer.

## RELIGION AND THE CAT

The early church knew about the link between cats and pagan religions. Rather than fight old beliefs and risk dissent, Christianity absorbed elements of the religions it replaced: St. Agatha of the second century was said to take the form of an angry cat to chastise women who worked on her saint's day. Very often the cat is found in pictures of the holy family, representing the "good cat" created to offset the creation of the devil's "evil mouse." Even the Virgin Mary was associated with the cat as the symbol of motherhood. An old Italian legend says a cat gave birth in the stable at the same moment as Mary. Early Christianity took the concept of the Virgin Mary and incorporated the cat fertility goddess' characteristics of love of children and chastity.

Muslims by all accounts seemed much enamored of cats. In A.D. 600, Muhammad preached with a cat in his arms, and there are several beautiful accounts of the Prophet's affection for the cat. A Muslim folktale asks, "Why do cats drink milk with their eyes closed?" and is answered, "So when asked by Muhammad if they've had any milk, cats can truthfully answer they've not seen any!"

© Scala/Art Resource, New York

## FALL FROM GRACE

The gods and angels of earlier religions become the demons of later ones. Many churchmen remembered the association of cats with pagan religion, and the "bad cat" became a popular scapegoat when religion sought to eradicate paganism.

Christianity taught its followers to regard their former deities as devils and to regard the followers of cat-gods as evil. The "Judas cat" that sits at the feet of Judas in paintings of the Last Supper is a far cry from the kitten found earlier with the Holy Family. The Church of Europe became the cat's worst enemy, encouraging cruel ceremonious killings of cats.

During the entire Middle Ages, the cat's favor continued to fall, until it was reviled as a treacherous, untrustworthy animal dedicated to evil. Although cats were often killed in the name of religion, it was also considered fine sport to torture cats. In Paris, cats in a bag were burned alive each St. John's Day to symbolically destroy evil. Another tradition consisted of throwing live cats from high places; this went on until after 1817. At her coronation in 1559, Queen Elizabeth I stuffed a number of cats into a wicker effigy of the Pope, then burned them.

The Old-English name for a tomcat was Gib or Gibbe-cat (hard "g"). This term is still used in parts of England and Scotland, and it seems to apply specifically to old, sorry-looking male cats.

MEDIEVAL LEGEND:  Trying to ape God and create a man, the Devil managed to produce only a sorry, skinless animal—the cat.  St. Peter felt sorry for the pitiful creature and gave it a fur coat—its one and only valuable possession.

By the thirteenth century, the Church needed a scapegoat to blame for the ills of the world, and it found witchcraft; the cat was an innocent bystander that was also persecuted.  Cats were often accused of being the "witches' familiar," and many a sad old woman was killed because of her kindness to a cat.  Because alleged witches were usually tortured, accused persons confessed to the witchcraft, solidifying society's beliefs and confirming that it was pursuing the right course of action.  The pandemonium spread to America, where the most infamous practices occurred in Salem, Massachusetts, in 1662.

During the Renaissance, the Catholic Church, by order of Pope Innocent VIII, decreed the destruction of all cats.  Thousands of cats were burned each month in England during the Middle Ages, until the practice was stopped by King Louis XIII in the 1630s.

## CAT CONTROL

The Church may have inadvertently caused, or at the very least, exacerbated the Great Plague epidemics of Europe.  Bubonic plague carried by flea-infested rats killed as many as fifty million people beginning in the fourteenth century in Europe.  Disease-infested rats ran rampant because there were too few cats to kill them.

## BACK ON THE PEDESTAL

By the middle of the seventeenth century, the French began welcoming cats back into polite society. Cardinal Richelieu kept dozens of them at court, and during the early eighteenth century, the French Queen of Louis XV and her contemporaries made it fashionable to keep pampered felines.

About the same time the cat was being welcomed back into hearts and homes, anticruelty societies were organized. British Parliament passed the first anticruelty law in 1822, and the world's first animal protection society was formed in 1824. When Queen Victoria became its patron in 1837, it became the Royal Society for the Prevention of Cruelty to Animals (RSPCA). The American SPCA soon followed in 1866, and ten years later the American Humane Association was founded.

Cats have been domesticated for at least five thousand years, but selective breeding did not really catch on until the mid-nineteenth century. The first recorded cat show was in St. Giles, Winchester, England, in 1598, but it was little more than a friendly gathering of cat fanciers putting their pride-and-joys on display. The first benched show was staged by Mr. Harrison Weir on July 13, 1871, at the Crystal Palace in London. This helped further the popularity of "pedigreed" cats, and showing and developing perfect examples of purebred cats became popular. The first American cat show was held in Madison Square Garden, New York City, in 1895; two hundred cats competed over a four-day period.

## CATS IN WAR

In 525 B.C. the Persian King Cambyses II was said to have defeated the Egyptian army by having his soldiers carry living cats as shields before them. The Egyptians refused to risk injuring a sacred cat and offered no resistance.

In 1535, in a report to the Council of One and Twenty at Strasbourg, an artillery officer reported that cats were used to dispense poisonous gas to the enemy. Poison bottles were strapped to their backs, and the cats were then sent into a panic-stricken run into the enemy camp.

During the siege of Stalingrad (Volgograd) during World War II, a cat named Mourka carried messages from a group of Soviet scouts back to company headquarters.

## RECENT CAT HISTORY

It hasn't been until the last fifteen or twenty years that cats have been afforded the same veterinary care available to other domestic animals. Previously, cats were treated like "miniature dogs." They were considered by most people to be merely a part of the barnyard menagerie—a self-sufficient little animal that needed little care.

In the early 1970s, cats began to gain in popularity, and a few veterinary practitioners followed the lead of Great Britain, which had become sensitive to cat care during the mid 1950s. Today, feline medicine is at the forefront of worldwide veterinary research and has been invaluable as a model for human medical advances.

The mid-1980s saw an explosion in the popularity of cats as pets. The United States cat population totals more than fifty-eight million, which is the largest population of cats in the world. There are currently about five million cats in Great Britain. Today, cats are kept in over thirty percent of households and have surpassed dogs as the number one pet of choice.

At long last, the cat has arrived.

THE EVOLUTIONARY CAT

## CHAPTER TWO

## THE CULTURED CAT

I look on the cat as a poem waiting to happen, its pause mere prologue to prankish delight, its purr a sweet river of song. A cat touches the soul. Wispy whisker-kisses, moist nosebumps—these are gifts beyond measure. To artists, a loving cat is an eternal muse. Writers seem to have an affinity for the feline, and the feeling appears to be mutual.

An early example of cats in literature is a verse by an anonymous ninth-century Irish monk, who worked as a manuscript copyist. He wrote a charming poem comparing the life of Pangur Ban to his own:

### TO PANGUR BAN, MY WHITE CAT

I and Pangur Ban my cat
'Tis a like task we are at;
Hunting mice is his delight
Hunting words I sit all night . . . .

One of the first writers to regularly include the cat in his work was the Greek writer Aesop. Later writers, like the English poet William Langland and the French writer La Fontaine, adapted Aesop's fables as the basis for stories that used the cat to advantage as both a political tool and moral device. Aesop's story "The Bell and the Cat" explores the problem of a domineering cat (the powers that be) playing with mice (common man). A proposed plan to "bell" the cat as an early warning device (kind of an ancient "Star Wars" system) is abandoned when no mouse will volunteer to place the bell. In "Venus and the Cat," a man is so besotted with his cat that Venus changes her into a beautiful woman. But the woman is unable to deny her true nature and springs from the marriage bed after a mouse and so is immediately turned back into a cat.

Poetry in the form of feline epitaph was a favorite literary form of many writers. A tenth-century Arab poet, Ibn Alalaf Alnaharwany, eulogizes a cat killed because of its habit of raiding the dovecote, bemoaning the fact that had the cat stayed with lesser fare of rats and mice, "thou hadst been living still, poor Puss."

In the nineteenth-century, Agnes Repplier dedicated one of her books to the memory of her cat, Agrippina. Queen Victoria's White Heather and Theodore Roosevelt's Tom Quartz both had biographies written about them.

Cat lovers throughout history have been torn by their love for the cat and their dislike of its enthusiastic war on birds. Benjamin Franklin wrote a very imaginative defense (in feline voice) on

"No favor can win gratitude from a cat."

La Fontaine

"The cat in gloves catches no mice."

Benjamin Franklin

"I am as melancholy as a gib-cat."

Falstaff (Shakespeare, *Henry IV*)

behalf of Madame Helvetius's cats to their mistress after the poor cats could not restrain their urge to plunder her birds.

Some stories, although appearing to be but a bit of whimsy, actually represent historical events. One such story, very old, called "Dick Whittington and his Cat", tells how Dick became Lord Mayor of London all because of a cat. Today, there is a memorial in London on Highgate Hill, called Whittington Stone, where tradition has it Dick Whittington heard Bow Bells calling him back to London. Richard Whittington really was Lord Mayor of London—three times (1397, 1406, and 1420)—and a statue of the famous cat sits atop the stone.

Perrault's adaptation of "The Master Cat" fables came about when he interwove characteristics of much older folk stories to create the famous "Puss in Boots," which first appeared in the 1697 Tales of Mother Goose. The youngest brother inherits Puss, a very clever talking cat. Through a series of ingeniously contrived situations, Puss is able to convince the king that his master is wealthy enough to merit the hand of the king's daughter.

Following the terrible Middle Ages when felines were brutalized, cats slowly became accepted again in England. Anthropomorphization became the vogue, and by the nineteenth century, the cat was being perceived as a "sly puss," rivaling the fox for its ingeniousness. Moralists and political satirists all took figurative aim at the cat, painting him as a villain or as merely rascally or stupid.

Later in the nineteenth century, the perception of cats became less stereotyped,

"Lat take a cat, and fostre him wel with milk,
And tendre flesh, and make his couche of silk,
An lat him seen a mous go by the wal;
Anon he weyveth milk, and flesh, and al,
And every deyntee that is in that hous,
Swich appetyt hath he to ete a mous."

Chaucer, "The Maunciple's Tale"

© Susanna Pashko/Envision

"Cats are a mysterious kind of folk—there is more passing in their minds than we are aware of."

Sir Walter Scott

"One of the most striking differences between a cat and a lie is that a cat has only nine lives."

Mark Twain

and all manner of good, bad, and indifferent cats were represented in literature. This seemed to herald a healthier cat attitude in general.

Edward Lear's 1871 edition of *Nonsense Songs* included the engaging poem-story of "The Owl and the Pussycat." Folklorists find all kinds of hidden meanings in the nonsense verse, wherein the owl and pussycat (both ancient deity figures) go to sea "in a beautiful pea-green boat" and are married, after which they "dance by the light of the moon." Edward Lear was also the inventor of the Runcible Cat and had a much-loved cat of his own in real life named Foss. Humorous sketches of Foss can be found throughout Lear's correspondence.

Following Lear's work, a host of stories written especially for children became the vogue. Beatrix Potter wrote and illustrated charming stories about Tom Kitten, Simpkin, and other kitties. Dr. Seuss produced The Cat in the Hat stories that continue to delight children (and adults) today.

Other authors represented the cat in a more serious vein. "The Cat that Walked by Himself" by Rudyard Kipling seeks to explain the very nature of the cat and in effect discounts that any "domestication" has occurred at all. It tells the story of the cat's original bargain made with the first woman. Cat agrees that he may sit inside by the fire and drink milk three times a day if he will kill mice and be kind to babies (as long as they do not pull his tail too hard). In all other ways, however, he remains "the Cat that Walks by Himself and all places are alike to him."

THE CULTURED CAT

Some of the most delightful cat stories are in the form of fairy tales for children. "The Boy Who Drew Cats" is an engaging Japanese tale, in which the cats painted on a screen come alive and slay the ogre, saving the life of the boy who painted them.

Another story set in Japan, "The Cat Who Went to Heaven," is a touching, uplifting children's tale by Elizabeth Coatsworth that has brought tears to many eyes—child and adult alike. A poor painter can scarce afford to feed himself, yet allows a pretty little cat called Good Fortune into his heart—and through his painting, Good Fortune is blessed and welcomed into heaven by the great Buddha Himself.

Cats inevitably reflected their former associations with the darker side of human nature and the occult. Algernon Blackwood kept many cats which may have helped inspire his decided gift for writing about the supernatural. Lilian Jackson Braun created the Siamese cat "Madam Phloi" as a recurring character in several mystery stories. A much more ominous and well-known example of the darker side is Edgar Allen Poe's "The Black Cat". Despite the grim tale, Poe was a great admirer of cats, and his

There used to be a kind of cheese made in Cheshire marked with a grinning cat face on one end. Is this where Lewis Carroll's wonderful Cheshire Cat came from?

tortoise-shell Catarina was a great comfort to him and often slept with his wife to help keep her warm as she lay dying of consumption. Many other writers were great cat enthusiasts, and often the cat was included in their work. Aldous Huxley's recommendation to aspiring psychological novelists was to obtain a pair of cats, preferably Siamese, and observe them. Other famous cat-loving writers included Lord Byron, the Brontë sisters and William Wordsworth. One cat actually wrote a book (Paul Gallico was kind enough to translate it from the feline) called *The Silent Miaow,* which is a handbook for cats (not their owners). This how-to book explains how, if you are a cat, you can control literally everything, without humans ever realizing it.

Charles Dickens had a cat called "The Master's Cat," and this engaging kitty would divert the writer's attention by snuffing out the candles with her paw. Mark Twain was a cat enthusiast and shared his house with four cats named Beelzebub, Blatherskit, Apollinaris, and Buffalo Bill. Harriet Beecher Stowe, creator of *Uncle Tom's Cabin,* lived in a house whose property adjoined Twain's. The Stowe and Twain cats often visited back and forth, and even "wrote" letters to each other.

No discussion of cats in literature would be complete without mention of Lewis Carroll's *Alice In Wonderland,* and the famous grinning Cheshire Cat. The Cheshire Cat expounds on the meaning of insanity, explaining to the dubious Alice that he is truly mad, because contrary to the dog, he growls when he's pleased, and wags his tail when he's angry.

A host of other well-known writers were cat lovers. Ernest Hemingway at one time kept twenty five cats in his house. He crossed Cuban cats with Angoras to produce what he incorrectly believed to be a new breed of cat. Henry James kept cats, and often had one shoulder draped with a favorite cat. The French writer and actress Colette was never found without a cat, and she declared "all our best friends are four-footed."

Other cat lovers/writers include May Sinclair, Edith Sitwell, Guy de Maupassant, Victor Hugo, Honoré de Balzac, Thomas Carlyle, William Faulkner, Damon Runyon, Baudelaire, John Keats, and Vachel Lindsay. All were devotees of the cat, and many wrote charming stories that included their favorite felines.

## THE "COMPOSED" CAT

Composers also include the cat in their works, often collaborating with literary cat lovers. Hans Verner Henze wrote an opera based on Balzac's *Loves of an English Cat,* and Igor Stravinsky composed a setting for Lear's "The Owl and the Pussycat."

The distinctive vocalizations of the cat have inspired many composers. Gioacchino Rossini has two female singers compete with variations on the word "meow" in "Duetto Buffo Deii Due Gatti." Another cat duet appears in Ravel's *L'Enfant et les Sortileges,* for which cat-lover Colette wrote the libretto. In Prokofiev's *Peter and the Wolf,* the cat character is easily identified by a clarinet theme throughout the work.

Even ballet is not immune to the wiles of the cat. Tchaikovsky's *Sleeping Beauty* has a wonderful *pas de deux* for a pair of fairy-tale cats; the orchestration not only imitates their "cat" calls but engineers a realistic feline "spit." But a piece composed truly for and by the cat is "Cat Fugue" by Domenico Scarlatti. The main musical theme was supposedly created by the composer's own cat walking across the piano keys.

"It is easy to understand why the rabble dislike cats. A cat is beautiful, it suggests ideas of luxury, cleanliness, voluptuous pleasures . . . etc."

Baudelaire, *Intimate Journals*

© Christopher Bain

Feline themes were not limited to the concert halls, however. The cat leaped into popular music of the eighteenth and nineteenth centuries, and publishers promoted numerous songs with colorful pictures of cats. Many of these songs poked fun at the amorous antics of cats and compared them to humans. "Me-ow Song," a 1919 comedy song by Harry D. Kerr and Mel B. Kaufman, tells of Angora and his evening escapades. Others songs mimicked kitty vocabulary à la Rossini, as in "Cat's Duet" by Berthold, where the only words are "Miau!"

It is appropriate that the cat, with all its foibles, and with society's varying perceptions of it, has long been celebrated in literature. The adaptation of T. S. Eliot's delightful *Old Possum's Book of Practical Cats* into Andrew Lloyd Webber's enormously successful musical *Cats* is indicative of just how far society's opinion has come.

Mark Twain said it best:

"A home without a cat—and a well-fed, well-petted and properly revered cat — may be a perfect home, *perhaps*, but how can it prove its title?"

*Cats have appeared in advertising for over 100 years, selling everything from Kaliko Kat Shoes to Tabby Cigars. Here, Thomas and Felice join in a fetching feline duo to celebrate the "superb blend" of Calvert's Whiskey.*

# Are Cats Musical?

Cat lovers and behaviorists agree that cats seem to respond to music—but their explanations remain at odds.

The French writer Théophile Gautier noted that although his kitty enjoyed listening to women singers, she hated high notes, especially high A. She used her paw to try to shut the woman's mouth whenever that particular note was reached.

Another critical cat belongs to flute teacher Sharon Northe. In a letter to *Cat Fancy* magazine, she says if the music is well done, Muffin begs to come into the music room, and basks in the sound of the flute. But whenever Sharon's flute students hit a wrong note, Muffin lets them know. "She puts her foot down—right on the student's foot—and scolds him or her with a commanding chorus of yowls." Muffin will even jump on the piano keyboard and try to drown out the bad sound.

Although it's hard to know whether cats listen to music for pleasure's own sake, it does seem clear that many cats are affected by and recognize specific music. The composer Henri Sauguet had a cat that reacted to Debussy's music as if it were catnip, rolling about on the carpet and licking the hands of whoever happened to be playing the piano. The journal of John Wesley notes that a lion and tiger at the Edinburgh Zoo were fond of flute music. Another cat cited by *Cat Fancy* magazine is Betty LaGow's cat, Smithers, who recognizes his favorite song, "The Atchison, Topeka, & the Santa Fe," and will come barreling straight to her whenever she sings or whistles it.

Some animal behaviorists conclude that cats are merely interpreting the music from their own background knowledge of cat sound signals. Cats, they say, mistake music as the sounds of other cats in distress, or the sounds of parental or sexual behavior, and react accordingly. Because there is such a wide range of reactions—varying from extreme to nothing at all—these specialists label the musical sense of cats as "just another feline myth."

But why shouldn't there be cats that, like humans, appreciate music, while others remain tone-deaf? There are certainly humans of both types—some are fine musicians, while others couldn't sing "Happy Birthday." Why should cats be different?

Take, for instance, a ragdoll kitty named Jeremy that lives with Gail A. Chmura in New Jersey. Apparently Jeremy can match with perfect "meow"-pitch any note Gail plays on the piano. Now, that sounds like true kitty musicality.

Many will be disappointed if it ever turns out that feline musical sense really is a myth. If that happens, please, don't tell Jeremy.

# Ailurophile or Ailurophobe

## FAMOUS CAT LOVERS AND HATERS

Although the Church was famous for persecuting kitty during the Middle Ages, a few individuals later championed the beleaguered feline. Pope Leo XII (1823-29) was very fond of cats, and had a large gray and red cat with black stripes called Micetto. He even placed terms in his will providing for the care of Micetto after his death. Another cat actually shared the dinner table with Pope Pius IX (1846-78). This cat, as befitting his owner's station, was a very polite fellow, and always waited patiently for the Pope to finish dinner before being served his own food—by the Pontiff himself.

Heads of state also enjoyed the company of cats. Cardinal Wolsey, chancellor of England during King Henry VIII's reign (1509-47), often shared his chair with a favorite cat during important audiences. When President Lincoln found three half-frozen cats while visiting the camp of General Grant during the Civil War, he adopted the forlorn trio on the spot. Winston Churchill and Lenin were both avid cat lovers, and Theodore Roosevelt's cat, Slippers, often attended White House dinners and state occasions. President Calvin Coolidge kept three pet cats, named Blackie, Tiger, and Timmie—and a canary. Timmie was the ultimate diplomat; he would allow the canary, named Caruso, to parade about on his back, and the bird would even snuggle down to sleep between his paws.

Ten Downing Street, the traditional home of the United Kingdom's prime ministers, has had a string of resident cats. Winston Churchill's cat, Nelson, came with him in 1940; Jock was given to Churchill on his eighty-eighth birthday after he had left Ten Downing Street. He was given room and board for life and was even remembered in the great man's will, with the stipulation that a marmalade cat remain in "comfortable residence" at Churchill's country house at Chartwell forever. Wilberforce, a black and white cat, was chosen from a shelter to be another official Downing Street mouser, and he served under four prime ministers until he was retired by Margaret Thatcher in 1986. Wilberforce died in 1988 at the age of fifteen.

The famous and notorious have also despised cats. Hitler hated cats, perhaps because of their historical implications of occult power—power he could not control! Alexander the Great was also a cat hater. President Eisenhower couldn't abide cats and gave his staff a standing order to shoot cats on sight. Napoléon was terrified of cats; an aide once discovered the great man screaming and hysterically flailing a tapestry with his sword in a frantic attempt to kill the cat he thought was hidden there.

Why do some people hate or feel terror at the sight of the cat? Certainly many may be physically allergic to the cat or perhaps have had an unfortunate feline experience. But for each person who endures allergy to keep a cat for love's sake, there are those who experience cold sweats at the mere sight of a cat, with no clear explanation why.

Is the dislike, or fear, due to the cat's innate ability to call its own shots, to refuse to give unquestioning loyalty? Maybe fear springs from the cat's unpredictability or his unsettling aura of "other-worldliness."

For me to understand the reasons for ailurophobia is as hard as explaining why I adore cats. I'm just glad to be on the right side.

# The Artistic Cat

People's fascination with cats fostered an early desire to celebrate and commemorate the cat in art. The earliest examples of kitty art appear in cave drawings and ancient amulets used by early cults that worshipped cats. Ancient Egyptian art includes murals found on the walls of ancient tombs, statues representing cat deities, and cat motifs on everyday utensils, clothing, and jewelry. The Brooklyn Museum has one of the best collections of ancient Egyptian art in the world.

Early on, the cat appeared in bestiaries and border decorations of manuscripts. Many of the paintings by Jacopo da Ponte (c. 1510-92) include what appears to be the same cat, which may have been a da Ponte family pet. Examples of cats as representational art abounded before and during the Middle Ages, when cats were used to represent good and, more often, evil or the devil. In Goya's etching/aquatint *Ensayos* (Trials), the cat familiar is present.

Cats are included in paintings of Christian imagery as well. Albrecht Dürer's engraving of Adam and Eve (1504) shows the "good cat" in the foreground ignoring the "evil mouse" because before the fall there were no adversaries. *The Garden of Heavenly Delights* by Hieronymus Bosch (c. 1450-1516) includes Adam and Eve, and a cat stalking off with a rat in its mouth.

Paintings of the Holy Family often include a cat. Leonardo da Vinci (1452-1519) painted *Madonna and Child with a Cat*, in which Jesus clutches the kitty in an attempt to keep it from escaping. Baroccio's painting of "Madonna of the Cat" (now in the National Gallery in London) is linked with the symbolism of the Virgin. However, cats were also often symbolically linked to the treachery of Judas, and paintings of the Last Supper often show a cat. Other masters that incorporated the cat in their work were Titian, Rubens, and Rembrandt, to name only a few.

Seventeenth-century engravings more often found cats as companions in portraits. Cats were included in the engravings of both Francis Barlow and Cornelius Visscher. In the eighteenth century, kitties appeared in paintings such as Hogarth's portrait of the Graham children.

© Shelburne Museum, Shelburne, VT

Minnie From the Outskirts of the Village, by *R.P. Thrall, 1876.*

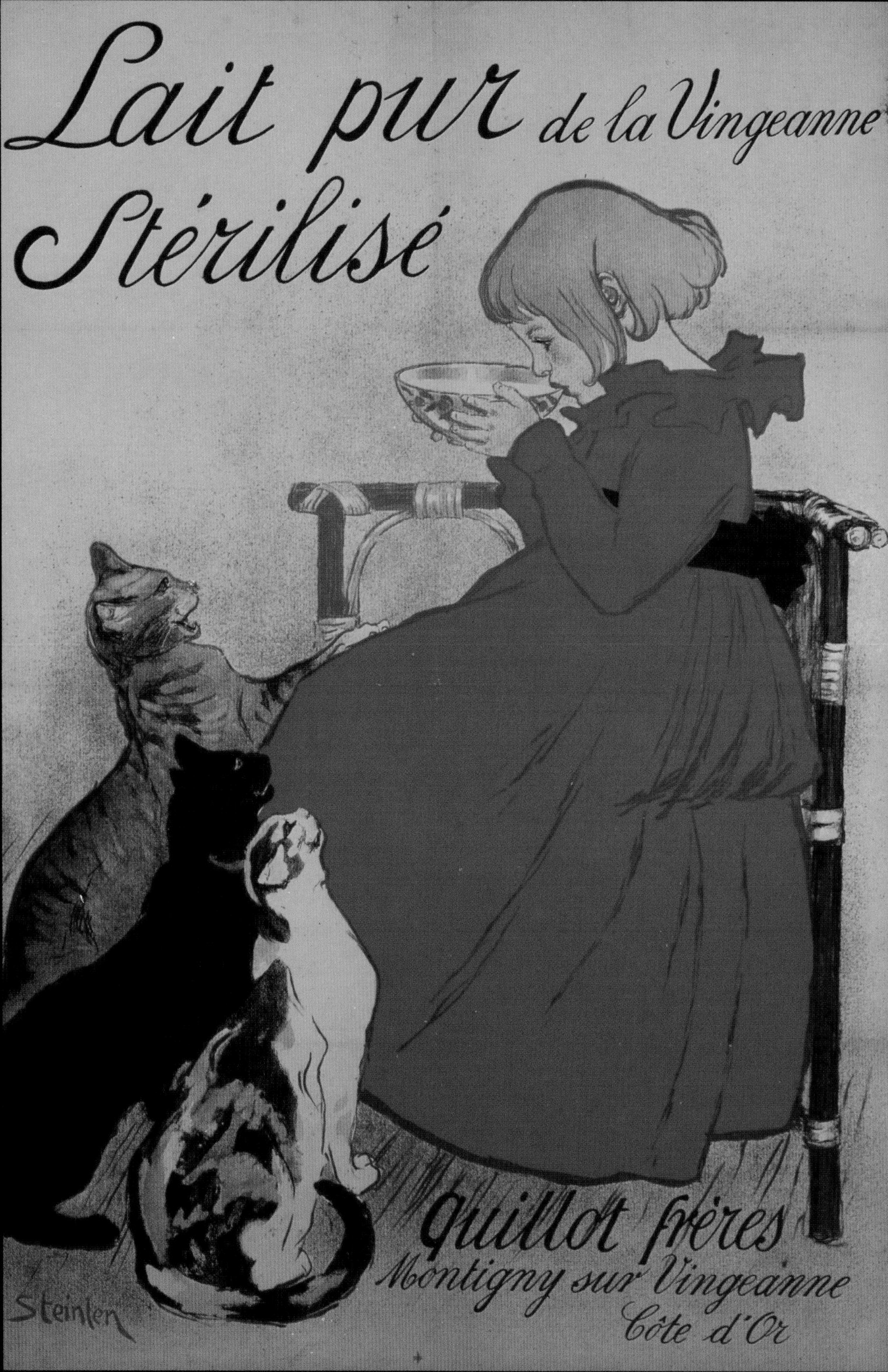


*Steinlen's poster* Lait Pur Stérilisé de la Vingeanne, *1894.*

Another example is the striking and endearing painting by Joseph Wright (1734-97) entitled *Dressing the Kitten,* in which two young girls fit a kitten with doll's clothing.

In the nineteenth century, traveling artists frequently featured cats by themselves or in the company of children. Artist Gottfried Mind became known as "the Raphael of Cats" for his love of cats. He was the first painter to specialize in cat portraits. In 1809, in Basel, the city where Mind lived, there was a suspected outbreak of rabies, and the destruction of all cats was ordered—Mind hid and saved his own beloved cat Minette, but mourned the loss of eight hundred of the city's cats.

Henriette Ronner (1821-1909) also was known for her paintings of cats and kittens. Renoir, Rousseau, Bonnard, Picasso, Dufy, Toulouse-Lautrec, and many other notables included cats in their works.

Swiss-born Theophile Alexandre Steinlen moved to Paris about a hundred years ago and became famous for his graphic renderings of cats. He worked as an illustrator for advertisements, and cats figured prominently in his posters. He would often stop to sketch any cat he saw— his house in Paris became known as "Cat's Corner." Today, reproductions of his work as posters and postcards remain among the most popular kitty art.

Paris even features two galleries devoted exclusively to cat art. One of these galleries, The Cat Enthroned, Card Shop-International Gallery of the Cat (Le Chat en Majeste, Carterie-Galerie Internationale du Chat) can be found not far from the Paris Opera. The European Gallery of the Cat is another cat lover's delight. Offerings include statues of cats in every medium and size and position, posters and postcards, and prints and paintings. Some of the most popular of today's cat artists are regularly featured in both of these galleries; they include Maxime Juan, who drew "Le Chat en Majeste," for which the gallery is named; J. Pathe-Lancry; Albert Decaris, who is lauded by some as the best for his etchings of cats; and Geri Wilde, an American artist. Cats play an important role in the work of another contemporary American artist, Will Barnett. He often includes his family cat, Madame Butterfly, in his works and recent silk screens almost exclusively feature the cat (and a parrot). His work is available through the Associated American Artists Gallery in New York City.

Cat lovers today have a plethora of kitty art from which to choose. These vary from colorful cartoons and reasonably priced prints to higher-priced portraits, paintings, and sculptures. Of course, the camera enables all of us to possess the most valuable feline artwork of all—a portrait of our own favorite kitty.

©Deanne Rosen

*Sylvie Gardyn owns the European Gallery of the Cat. She holds a poster advertising her gallery and shop, which offers many feline treasures.*

*The gates of San Marco, Venice, Italy.*

# Sign of the Cat

The sign of the cat has always figured prominently in coats of arms. Heraldry used the lion, wildcat, and domestic cat as symbols of ferocity, might, and threat: the British Lion represented Britannia's power; the city of Coventry featured a cat signifying watchfulness; the Dutch chose the cat as their sign for its love for, and fierce defense of, liberty. The motto of the Mackintosh family is "touch not the cat, but (without) a glove," and its crest is a mountain cat.

Many heraldic signs were chosen as puns and plays on words; hence, the name Archer is represented by three arrows; Butler by tankards of wine; Hunter by greyhounds. The family crest of the German family Katzen was a silver cat holding a mouse on an azure field. Most of the old clan of Chattan adopted the mountain cat as their crest. The village sign of Old Catton uses the figure of a cat perched on a barrel, or tun, as it was known to form the rebus "cat + tun = Catton."

Later, the cat came to be a symbol of evil, and its use by nobility was suspended. When Catholicism suffered disfavor during Protestant rule in England, the cat was depicted as sitting at the feet of a Pope, showing treason and hypocrisy.

Although the cat was scorned by the nobility, its popularity continued among simple shopkeepers and merchants. The Cat in Boots remained a favorite emblem of the bootmakers' guild, and to this day in England, the Cat and the Fiddle appears as a familiar sign for a village inn.

# Working Cats

From the beginning, cats have earned their keep sweeping farms and buildings clean of mice and rats. Although cats often "do their duty" as a matter of course, many notable felines have actually been placed on the payroll.

Newspaper Row was famous for keeping cats. The cats of *The Sun*, published in New York from 1833 to 1928, were described by their editor Charles Dana, as *Felis domestica; var., journalistica*. At the end of the nineteenth century, The Century Company installed a cat to keep mice from chewing off the backs of magazines. Century, as the cat was, of course, named, was paid in meals of beef or mutton, and his weekly account was even audited with the general business of the magazines.

Cats are found in many stables, not only hunting vermin, but also becoming fast friends with the horses. Other cats are part of medical "kitty therapy" programs, benefiting human patients immeasurably.

*Cat Fancy* magazine says some cats earn their keep as "enforcers." Grand Prairie Police Reserve of Grand Prairie, Texas, has the "biggest, baddest" cat the local shelter could provide—a twenty-pound white long-haired cat called Fang who purrs whenever visitors make an appearance,

Ships' cats had their own signal to return to the ship before they pulled out to sea—the half-hour whistle called the crew, the fifteen-minute toot alerted stragglers, and the five-minute trill summoned the cats. The ships whistles were halted during World War II, and, sadly, cats were marooned all over the world.

although he is supposed to guard the property room. Another kitty called Donut even has a security badge; he works as a security cat for Lockheed Shipbuilding Company.

Around the world cats fulfill duties in churches, libraries, post offices, and hotels. The Cat System of the British Post Office, which began in the autumn of 1868, supports the upkeep of mousers to this day, passing the duties from dad-cat to son-cat. Hamlet was a well-known resident of the Algonquin Hotel in New York. Towser worked as chief mouser on the staff of Scotland's oldest distillery, achieving a world record total "kill" in his lifetime of 28,899 mice. Mike held court at the gates of the British

The first television star was Felix the Cat. He was the first image to be experimentally transmitted in the 1920s. Drawn by cartoonist Otto Messmer, Felix is often more notably associated with Pat Sullivan of Paramount Studios, for whom Messmer worked.

Since Felix, many cartoon cats have careened and caterwauled over the airwaves and big screen. They've included such notables as Top Cat; The Cat in the Hat; Tom of Tom & Jerry; Sylvester Puddytat; Jim Davis's Garfield; and all the kitties of Disney's *Oliver and Company* and *Aristocats*.

Museum for twenty years, and a 165-page obituary was published upon his death.

Whatever their duties, cats have a knack for taking center stage—some more literally than others. Tanna the Singing Cat is the official greeter at a recording studio in Irving, Texas, and she's even made her own record. The Bristol Opera House's theater cat Groegheist (Gray Ghost) often disappeared before a performance; the audience was always delighted when he later made his entrance as an unrehearsed, yet totally natural, member of the cast. Princess Kitty, a former stray turned actress, lives with her friend and trainer, Karen Payne. Princess played Ernest Hemingway's favorite cat in a television miniseries starring Stacy Keach—who has eleven cats of his own.

*Rhubarb* (1951) won the first Picture Animal Top Star Award (PATSY) from the American Humane Association. The cats in *Breakfast at Tiffany's* (1962) and Tonto in *Harry and Tonto* (1985) were also PATSY winners, and the famous finicky Morris won the coveted award in 1973. A gorgeous chinchilla named Solomon appeared in *You Only Live Twice* and *Diamonds Are Forever,* both James Bond movies. Midnight, the black cat wearing a diamond studded collar in the introductions to the television series "Mannix" and "Barnaby Jones," won the PATSY in 1974.

Other cat movies have had great success: In Disney's *The Incredible Journey,* based on a book by Sheila Burnford, a Siamese cat named Tao and two dogs travel two hundred miles to return home; *The Cat from Outer Space,* written by Ted Key, is a sci-fi fantasy about an alien cat named Jake stranded on earth; *That Darn Cat!* stars a seal point called D.C. (for Darn Cat) that helps an FBI agent catch a couple of criminals; and *The Three Lives of Thomasina* is based on the book by Paul Gallico.

For most of us, the cat in our life is a star—and we wouldn't think of asking them to work. We know in our heart-of-hearts that our kitty is as talented and beautiful as any of the celebrated cats on the silver screen. It doesn't matter if anyone else ever sees them there—it's enough that they shine for us.

*Morris, the eccentric "spokes-cat" for 9-Lives foods, poses for the camera. He is probably the most famous working cat today. The original Morris, "discovered" in an animal shelter, died in 1978. Morris' carefully chosen look-alike successor continues to fill the great cat's decidedly finicky shoes.*

# Cat Lore and Legend

Cat history is cloaked in myth and superstition. Our ancestors searched for answers to the questions of the existence of the cat and often came up with entertaining and eloquent explanations. One such legend gives as good an explanation as any of the creation of the cat.

Hebrew folklore says cats didn't exist before the Flood. Noah was very concerned there might be trouble between the lion and the other creatures on the ark, and he prayed to heaven for help. God answered, and sent the lion into a deep, deep slumber. Seeing this, Noah was relieved. But later, Noah became concerned that rats would be as dangerous a problem as the lion—what if they ate all the provisions? Again, Noah begged the Lord to send him a way to fight this calamity, and again, the Lord answered Noah's prayer. The lion, in the midst of his slumbers, made a great sneeze—ACHOO!— and out of the sneeze came a pretty little cat.

"Creation" fables are numerous, as are legends that answer other questions of life. One tells of a contest between Sun and Moon to see who could create the best animals. Sun created the lion, and the other gods oohed and aahed. Their admiration for the lion filled Moon with envy. In answer, Moon caused a nimble little cat to spring from the earth. But Sun and the other gods laughed at such a poor "imitation lion" and there was much merriment in the heavens. Sun countered Moon's attempt by creating the mouse as a sign of his contempt. In desperation, Moon tried again, and created a monkey; but the monkey was greeted with even more hilarity. Moon was so embarrassed and angered by the mockery her creations aroused, that she caused an eternal hatred to spring between the creatures. To this day, the lion hates the monkey, and the cat detests the mouse—and all because Sun laughed at Moon.

An early Christian folktale tells how, when the baby Jesus was unable to sleep, the Madonna begged the animals in the stable to help Him to slumber. Sadly, none were successful. Then, a little striped gray kitten padded forward (after first thoroughly licking herself clean) and looked shyly upon the Child. She hopped up and snuggled down beside Him, and began to purr a lullaby—and Baby Jesus promptly fell asleep. From that day forward, (so the legend tells), all proper tabby cats wear an "M" on their foreheads, as reminder of the kind service performed for the Madonna.

Muslims include cats in stories about the Prophet. One day when Muhammad was meditating, his cat Muezza lay down on the sleeve of his coat. Because Muhammad was very still during his contemplation, Muezza fell asleep. Later, when Muhammad had completed his mediation and was ready to arise, he saw the cat sleeping on his sleeve. Not wishing to disturb the perfect picture of the little cat's slumber, Muhammad took scissors and cut off the sleeve of his coat.

*This painting (c.1400 BC) found on a tomb wall in Thebes shows kitty playing retriever when its master Nebamun goes bird hunting.*

## CATS AND GODS

Ancient Egypt wasn't alone in having cat deities. In Ireland, a cat-headed god was worshiped during the first century A.D., and cats are still considered to be conversant with the "little people" (leprechauns) in Ireland. A huge black cat called Iruscan, the King of the Cats, figures in Irish folklore. It was believed that even the close proximity of a tortoiseshell cat aided the development of second sight, and children were encouraged to play with them. Today, it's still an Irish and Scottish belief that tortoiseshell cats bring good fortune.

Freya, the Viking goddess of Love and Beauty, rode in a chariot drawn by the most affectionate of all domestic animals, the cat. Freya was given power over the "nineth world"— some historians speculate this might be an allusion to the nine lives that cats are supposed to have.

In China, Li Chou was a fertility god worshiped in cat form, to whom sacrifices were offered at the end of the harvest. Sacrificial cats were not rare; often, the cat would be killed as the last sheaf of corn was reaped. In the Ardennes region of Western Europe, on the first Sunday of Lent, cats were burned and flocks driven through the smoke as a protection against witchcraft. In Eastern Europe, cats were buried alive in the cornfield to ensure a good harvest, and in some parts of France, it was believed that burying a kitten in the garden prevented the growth of weeds. Cats were often included in the foundations or walls of buildings as a charm to prevent rats.

*Sorcery—from a drawing by A.B. Frost. A witch conjures evil, while feline familiars watch.*

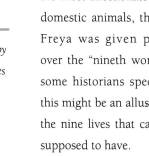

Northwind Picture Archives

## BAD CATS

The cat's padding feet have followed a twisty, torturous trail through history. One of the earliest superstitions affirms that a cat will steal breath from a sleeping child. This fear stems from a belief—probably fostered by Hebrew folklore—that cats are vampires. The Semitic witch-queen Lilith was Adam's first wife. Lilith refused to obey Adam and flew away, later becoming a vampire. Lilith is able to assume the form of a huge black cat named El Broosha, and human newborns are her favorite prey.

Traditionally, a witch's familiar ate by sucking blood from the body—another vampiristic legend. Cats were often thought to be familiars. In fact, witch's cats were thought to possess all sorts of terrible powers; their teeth were venomous, flesh poisonous, their hair would cause suffocation if swallowed, and their breath would infect human lungs with consumption (tuberculosis). Cats made beer go sour and cows run dry and they carried souls to the devil.

Some believed that the witch's familiar was the devil or perhaps an evil "imp" sent by the devil to instruct and inspire the witch. Others held that the witch could actually assume the shape of any animal she chose, and that the familiar was actually the witch in cat form. Many believed witches were granted the power to use the body of familiars and could "possess" their cats nine times—yet another allusion to the nine lives of the cat.

There is an ancient Celtic belief that kittens born in May should be killed, because they bring snakes into the house. An old Huntingdonshire proverb says,

*"May chets bad luck begets and
sure to make dirty cats"*

In Europe and early America, black cats were particularly feared, because black was the color of the night and darkness, associated with the devil and evil. But before the advent of the witch's familiar, China was the only culture with specific superstition against a black cat. In China, the approach of a black cat was believed to be an omen of sickness or poverty.

# GOOD CATS

The colors of a cat's fur have sealed its fate, certain shades being more auspicious than others. Sir John Denham, a seventeenth-century poet, supports the color theory in the following verse (probably the terms "fat" and "lean" are used metaphorically to mean "prosperous" or "poor"):

*"Kiss the black cat,
And that'll make ye fat:
Kiss ye the white one
And that'll make ye lean."*

© George Mattei/Envision

In a somewhat backhanded "good cat" superstition of the Middle Ages, a cat that crossed your path without doing you harm was very good luck. Britain had a long-standing tradition that a black cat crossing your path or entering your house was good luck. A black cat was also supposed to be able to cure epilepsy.

Ancient Egyptian tomb inscriptions document the belief that the cat was a bringer of prosperity and health, long life, and beautiful old age. A Buddhist superstition holds that a light-colored cat ensures silver will always be in the house and that a dark-colored cat ensures gold. A tricolor cat supposedly protects a house from fire, and a double-clawed cat (see page 71) is a very potent bringer of good fortune and should be guarded and preserved.

## CATS AND AFTERLIFE

In Ancient Babylon, it was believed that the cat acted as the host for certain holy human souls after death, for the rest of the cat's natural life; only in this way could the departed soul gain Paradise. The Buddhist, Burmese, and Siamese cultures had similar beliefs. In ancient Japan, certain cats were believed to hold the soul of an ancestor and were jealously guarded as priceless.

## CATS AND MARRIAGE

Gods of the past were often associated with fertility or virginity, which explains why cats are thought to bring luck in marriage. French folklore says a strange white cat mewing on a doorstep foretells a speedy marriage. In Southern England, owning a black cat ensures the daughters of the house will get married. Other parts of England hold that a black cat is a lucky wedding gift. If a cat sneezes within the bride's hearing on her wedding day or eve, good luck will come to her. But woe betide the maiden that steps on a cat's tail—she won't marry that year.

## CATS AND THE WEATHER

Cats were believed to have the ability to influence the weather, and particularly storms at sea. A light breeze that ripples the water during a calm, which indicates a coming squall, is still known as a cat's-paw.

Other superstitions state that cats can actually provoke, rather than predict, changes in the weather. In many countries, bathing a cat or immersing it in water is thought to induce rain. By playing with a string, kitty stirs a tempest, and a playing cat is believed to foretell a gale or actually to cause it. Scots and Japanese believe tortoiseshell cats can foretell storms: Both countries believe a cat crying in the night indicates a storm; in Scotland, a cat scratching table or chair legs is "raising wind"; and a Japanese cat is foretelling rain if it cleans itself behind its ears with a wet forepaw. Because bolts of lightning were designed by angels to rid cats of the evil spirits that infest them during thunderstorms, in Scotland cats are kicked outside to keep the house from being hit.

## EXTRASENSORY PERCEPTION

The incredible sensory machine of the cat makes human abilities pale in contrast. Humans, compared to cats, are blind, deaf, and without feeling or scent sense. It must seem to our kitties that their poor upright companions walk around with bags over their heads. Is it any wonder we are both terrified and enchanted by the amazing abilities our cats seem to possess?

THE CULTURED CAT

Despite the current so-called "enlightened age," cats cling to their occult reputations of old. However, Desmond Morris, noted zoologist and author of *Catwatching* and *Catlore,* is adamant in his belief that cats have no supernatural powers, and that if a cat's unusual action is unexplainable today, it will be scientifically understood tomorrow.

Many superstitions of the past have been explained by today's scientific knowledge. Cats are highly sensitive to vibrations, and often give warning of an imminent earthquake ten to fifteen minutes before it strikes. Peasants who live on Mt. Etna keep cats as early warning devices. Cats also seem able to sense and alert owners to air raids before the sirens are sounded—again, the vibrations of the planes most likely are felt long before humanly detectable. The association of cats with weather is also quite understandable; we know today that the fine-tuned senses of a cat are able to detect variation in barometric pressure and that subsequent behavioral changes could predict a shift in the weather.

But, as all cat lovers know, many things about your pet just can't be explained.

# PSI-TRAILING

Psi-trailing is a term coined to describe the apparent ability of some cats to find their way home over long distances. This ability is celebrated in the story, *The Incredible Journey,* by Sheila Burnford, of a Siamese cat named Tao who leads furry companions two hundred fifty miles (402 km) across the country to be reunited with their family. One of the best-documented cases is of a veterinarian's cat, identified by a bone growth on the fourth vertebrae of his tail; the cat left New York and found his owner, who had moved to California. Another cat, Pooh, had a scar on his side and

an unusual black spot on his foot; he walked two hundred miles (322 km) four months to rejoin his family, which had moved from Georgia to South Carolina. Chat Beau's owners identified him by the scar on one eye, and his habit of growling like a dog, after he trailed his family to Texas, three hundred miles (483 km) and four months away from Louisiana. Sugar was identified by a deformed left hip joint after arriving in Oklahoma from California—traveling fifteen hundred miles (2,414 km) in fourteen months. Skeptics will never be convinced, but believers cannot be dissuaded of the many instances in which beloved felines somehow turned up to rejoin their families.

# WHAT TIME IS IT?

The cat's time sense is also extraordinary. In the past, kitty has mystified man by reliably knowing the time of day certain events occur. To a certain extent we can understand time sense. But what about the cat's ability to know in advance about a change in routine, when even the human remains unaware? For instance, if your family feline races to the front door thirty seconds before the kids' school bus arrives every day (not at all unusual behavior), how does she know when the bus is early or late? Many skeptics say the cat is able to identify a bus or a familiar car long before humans are able to, and that this is easily explainable behavior having nothing to do with ESP, but with hearing.

But some cats seem to have this ability when sense of hearing can have nothing to do with the phenomena. The cat Mysouff belonging to the famous French writer Alexandre Dumas was known to be psychic; not only did it unerringly meet Dumas at an appointed place and time each afternoon, but if he was going to be late, the cat would know and not bother to leave the house.

## GHOSTS AND CATS

The belief that cats have a link with the "other world" is widely held. The popular movie *Ghost* features a cat that is able to see the spirit of the murdered victim, played by Patrick Swayze. "Track the spook," a behavior of watching things that aren't there is often shown by cats, lending credence to this belief. The cat will fix its gaze on a point in mid-space between the eye and the nearest object, and "watch" the something move—across the room, up the wall, around the ceiling, and out the door. Is it an actual presence, an infinitesimal object, or a sound our own ears cannot detect?

A letter to the *Occult Review* of April 1924 tells of a ghost that appeared in a chair. A cat in the room immediately jumped into the spirit's lap and was dismayed to discover the insubstantial lap would not hold it!

In some instances, it appears that the great love and respect we share with our companion cats lives beyond the grave. There are countless stories of cats wailing at the exact instant of a beloved owner's death or the tracks of never-seen mourning "ghost cats" left at the grave site.

## CAT GHOSTS

Spirit-cats often seem to return to beloved owners after death—or at least, a photographable image returns. In 1925, a family portrait taken by Major Allistone in Clarens, Switzerland, revealed a surprise. The photo included a woman restraining a baby from climbing out of its carriage, with an older boy standing in front holding a stuffed rabbit in his left hand. In his right hand, the face of a white kitten appeared—only the kitten had died several weeks before, mauled by a St. Bernard! Examinations of the negative proved that the kitten was actually there. In 1974, a photo taken by Alfred Hollidge in Essex, England, of a live cat named Monet revealed an "extra" catlike form which Monet seems to be watching.

Do our pets really return in ghostly form? Or do our own wishes make it so? Either way, the evidence is extraordinary, and raises eerie questions with no ready answers.

No other creature in history has inspired man to the extent of the mysterious cat. There's no point making fun of people that take comfort in believing these harmless "kitty tales," especially since conclusive proof on either side of the coin is hard to find. Perhaps down the road we'll come to understand such unique experiences, but until that time, such matters are better left undiscussed with those who are so touched by the cat. Someday, as Mr. Morris believes, such phenomena will surely be understood.

But even if Mr. Morris' hypothesis proves true, that does not make the cat's mysterious abilities any less extraordinary.

## The Active Cat

# THE PHYSICAL CAT

A cat is a marvel of engineering.  Anyone who has ever observed one for any length of time will attest to its amazing flexibility.  Cats have very elastic bodies, in part because their spines are held together by muscles instead of ligaments, as in the human body.  Cats are so muscular they can move their spines by as much as 180 degrees.  A cat has seven cervical, thirteen thoracic, seven lumbar, and three sacral vertebrae—five more vertebrae than you do.  In addition, there are another twenty-one caudal vertebrae in the tails of most cats.  A cat's skeleton is made up of approximately 244 bones, which is about one-fifth more in total than humans.  The extra bones are mostly in the spine and tail.

Kitty's shoulder blades are on its sides, not its back like a human's. The unique shoulder joints allow the forelegs to turn in nearly any direction and are attached to the chest only by muscles, not by a collarbone.  A narrow chest and

In 1950, a four-month-old kitten followed climbers to the top of the Matterhorn, to become the highest climbing kitty on record.

the absence of a collarbone help the cat twist and turn and give it a longer stride in running.

Cats are *digitigrade*; that is, they walk on their toes, which also makes for longer strides. Cats walk with minimum expenditure of energy. They move limbs on each side of the body together, so that the hind feet fall into the tracks left by the front feet, leaving a single irregular track.

Domestic cats can run about thirty-one miles per hour. The cat's tail acts as a counterbalance, like the pole a tightrope walker uses, and also as a counterweight for making quick turns at high speeds.

Cats can dash up trees as fast as they can run on the ground. Most domestic cats are expert climbers, but because of the curve of their claws, many find it easier to go up than to come down. The cat that gets "stuck" up a tree would rather yowl and yodel for human rescue than submit to an extremely undignified tail-first descent.

© Susanna Pashko/Envision

## THE HUNTING INSTINCT

The instinct to hunt is innate in all cats, but the ability must be learned by watching and practice. A cat instinctively recognizes certain "cues" in the hunted animal, such as the indentation of the neck, the texture of feather or fur, and running prey or prey "gone to ground" in a tiny hole. The fur cue is such a significant one that owners often find their cats "trigger" on fur-trimmed coats and chew them to pieces. Other cats may ignore a mouse until it moves. Often, a cat will forego easy prey to "fish" with a paw down a hidey-hole where it has seen a mouse disappear.

## SLEEPING

Cats sleep sixteen hours a day, and seventy percent of that time is spent in light catnaps. During naps, the kitty brain continues recording scents and sounds and comes instantaneously awake whenever its senses trigger an alarm. Only thirty percent of cat sleep is deep; the deep phase includes kitty dreams, where paws and claws twitch, whiskers move, and ears flick.

## THE CAT'S EYE

FABLE  At night, cats' eyes cast out the light they imbibe during the day, causing a bright shine.

FACT  The night "shine" of cats' eyes is caused by the *tapetum lucidum,* a layer of cells backing the retina. The tapetum is like a mirror, and increases vision by reflecting light back through the retina. When light escapes, we see "glow-in-the-dark" kitty eyes.

Cats' eyes have fascinated us for centuries. Whether gold or blue, green or copper, the beauty and mystery of the feline gaze causes even the most casual cat fan to wonder, "What is it they see?"

As in most carnivores, the feline eye is placed toward the front of the face. This almost doubles the hunter's chances of locating prey by providing a nearly 280-degree area of three-dimensional vision. Felidae possess the largest eyes of all carnivores. If human eyes were proportionally the same size as the cat's, they would be approximately eight inches in diameter.

The cat's eyes are positioned in "open orbits." The bony eye socket doesn't form a complete ring around the eye but remains open, to allow greater movement of the jaw.

Domestic cats' eyes use nearly fifty percent more available light than ours do, and need only one-sixth the illumination level. A cat sees when light passes through the pupil (black center of the eye) and is focussed by the lens behind it onto the retina at the back of the eye. Here, light signals are collected by the rods and cones, or receptors, located on the surface of the retina: rods respond to light; cones respond to color. Cats have a far greater number of rods than we do. The receptors send signals through the optic nerve to the brain, where sight is interpreted.

The lens of the cat's eye generally doesn't focus nearly as well as the human's. A cat's near vision isn't very good, which is why kitty sometimes has trouble locating food fallen from the bowl. A cat's peripheral vision is clearer than looking straight ahead.

The iris is the beautiful colored portion of the cat's eye that regulates how much light passes through. The iris is a figure-eight muscle mechanism, inflexible along the vertical axis, which spreads (dilates) the pupil sideways to a black circle that seems to engulf the iris, or squeezes it shut

In the eyes of large- to medium-sized cats, the pupil is like the human's—circular, contracting to a pinpoint. Pupils of wildcats and most of the genus *Felis* (including house cats) contract to perpendicular slits. The clouded leopard is unique, for it is midway between the two, its pupil shutting to an oblong shape.

© David C. Bitters/Photo/Nats

Nineteenth-century China told time by the dilation of cats' eyes. They believed cats' eyes grew narrower until twelve noon when they became like a fine line, and then began to widen again.

*"Odd-eyed" cats have a peculiar charm all their own. Congenital deafness sometimes occurs in white cats with blue eyes; this kitty may be deaf on the blue-eyed side.*

© Pat Scheibel

to a perpendicular slit. The cat's iris is able to open wider and shut much tighter than a human's. By constricting in bright sunlight and opening wide in the dark, the iris makes the most of available light.

## DO CATS SEE IN COLOR?

Yes, cats most definitely see in color; however, they probably don't use or appreciate color the way humans do. Cats see many more shades of gray than we do. Cats are also probably more sensitive to the ultraviolet end of the spectrum, which means they may be seeing colors we can't. Remember that, the next time kitty stares eloquently into space, at . . . nothing?

Although feline eyes have fewer cones (color receptors) than human eyes, cats do have the "equipment" to perceive color. However, until the 1960s, scientists couldn't prove the cat's ability to distinguish colors. Then, studies conducted by R. F. Ewer demonstrated that cats can tell the difference between red and green, red and blue, red and gray, green and blue, green and gray, blue and gray, yellow and blue, and yellow and gray.

Even so, it takes cats a long time to understand the concept of color. As many as 1,750 experiments were conducted before some cats realized their understanding of color was being tested! Then once they understood the concept, cats had the potential to become color connoisseurs.

Because cats normally don't use color in their day-to-day lives, Ewer speculates kitties literally must "train their brains" to translate color into meaning. This hypothesis leads him to the conclusion that cats can see color—they just don't care about it.

## THE HAW

Cats have a third eyelid called the "nictitating membrane," or haw, which is located beneath the two outer eyelids. The haw is pinkish/gray tissue that generally remains lowered in the inside corner. It isn't part of the light control mechanism but serves for added protection and lubrication. It may move from the inside corner horizontally across to the outside edge of the eye, remaining raised in cats that are not well (a good warning sign of ill health).

## SOUND SENSE

As predators, most cats ambush when they hunt. The cat's greater ability to hear very high pitches at great distances helps it pinpoint delicate sounds made by mice or other prey and helps make the cat a superb hunter.

Most cats have large ears that swivel 180 degrees. The movement of the external portion of the ear, called the *pina*, collects and directs sound waves into the auditory canal. Here, the sound waves strike the eardrum, setting the fragile membrane into sympathetic vibration. This vibration of the eardrum is amplified by the mechanism of the inner ear, which is composed of a complicated set of tiny bones and fluid-filled tubes. The amplified sound waves are transmitted as signals to the brain, where they are interpreted.

Cats can't hear the low tones that humans can, but they can outhear us in higher ranges, which may explain why cats respond to higher-pitched voices more readily. Young cats hear better than older ones, and in their prime cats may hear the higher pitched sounds of mice up to 60,000 cycles per second. (Humans in the best of situations hear only about 20,000 cycles per second.) Precision hearing fades with age. Cats older than five years (still young by most standards) tend to lose this exceptional ability, and thus the "edge" they had when younger.

## HOW DO CATS LAND ON THEIR FEET?

Cats have an uncanny sense of balance that is intrinsically tied to balance organs (the vestibular apparatus) of the inner ear. These organs provide the cat with split-second information, allowing it instantly to distinguish up from down, and to determine acceleration.

Dr. Mark Berkley, a professor of neuroscience and physics at Florida State University, designed a box that invites kitty exploration. A computer projects an image to either side of a screen, and kitty bumps a plexiglass panel on the corresponding side (either the right or left side) to indicate "yes, I see that," and is rewarded with food. Dr. Berkley concludes from these studies that cats can't tell the difference between human faces, that they have relatively poor color sense, and that they can experience visual illusion.

This great location sense coupled with the incredible flexibility and muscle control of the spine gives the cat the ability to fall on its feet. The cat determines which direction is up and how fast it is going and with a series of quick contractions of the spine, shoulders, and flanks simply turns itself in the air!

Cats lacking this inner ear apparatus are still able to land on their feet—but not if they are blindfolded. Therefore, cats probably rely on a combination of eyesight and equilibrium for the falling reflex to function.

When a cat lands, it arches its back and extends the legs to cushion the landing. Even in an "all-fours" landing, a cat can still crack his chin and split its palate—or break its legs. Some falls (as from the arms of a child) may not give the cat time to right itself.

Bickers has a right to mutter; he was thrown from the window of a moving car. He tried to land kitty-correct, but instead made a three-point landing—hind feet, front feet, and face. "He looked terrible. His nose and chin were all scabbed up," Christie Billingslea says of the cat she rescued. Bickers was lucky; he lost a little fur and a lot of dignity, but he gained a caring benefactress.

Falls from greater heights, such as those from balconies and windows of apartments, result in milder injuries. This is probably because the cats have time to fully relax and "parachute" the body, slowing the velocity of the fall before impact.

## SCENT SENSE

If we couldn't enjoy the inviting aroma of a Thanksgiving dinner or the fragrance of a delicate perfume, we would be disappointed but not terribly disgruntled. For us, smell is a source of pleasure, and an important factor in taste. Cats, on the other "paw," rely on an incredible olfactory ability, which is probably more important to a cat than hearing and sight combined.

The cat's nasal cavities are filled with bony plates (turbinals) against which airborne scent particles (pheromones) are tested. The turbinals are covered by a thick, spongy membrane (olfactory mucosa) composed of olfactory cells. A human being has five to twenty million such cells; a cat has sixty-seven million. Compared to cats, humans are scentblind. Imagine how frustrating it must be for a cat to sift through human colognes, cigarette smoke, and car fumes to enjoy the really important odors—like dinner.

Cats use scent in mating, to recognize food, and to identify friend and foe. Cats also use their scent sense to mark and identify territory. Cats use scent glands in the lips (perioral gland), chin (submental organ), forehead (temporal gland), and tail (caudal gland) by rubbing against objects or other cats in greeting. When Tom winds about your ankles or lovingly rubs cheeks with you, be flattered; he thinks enough of you to actually mark you as his personal possession. Without that marked scent, your kitty couldn't tell you from the lady down the street.

Theophile Gautier's cat, Mme. Theophile, loved the scent of shawls stored in sandalwood boxes; another cat named Seraphita "with little spasms of pleasure bit handkerchiefs impregnated with scent."

Cats have a second scent-detecting organ called the vomero-nasal organ (Jacobson's organ). It's in the roof of the mouth between the nose and the palate. Pheromones are transferred to the organ when kitty typically lifts its upper lip and wrinkles its nose in a grimacing inhalation, called "flehmen." Jacobson's organ doesn't connect to the olfactory area of the brain. Scientists believe it triggers motivation for feeding and sexual behavior.

Cats often use smell as a means of recreation. Scent identifies life for the cat—without it, he would be lost.

*Cats identify each other by smell, first engaging in friendly nose bumping, and then anal sniffing. Kitty often tries to do the same with a human, first bumping noses, then turning around to present a tail held high for the obligatory sniff. Even though it insults the cat, most humans decline the invitation.*

Catnip is not a feline aphrodisiac and will not bring on heat in a female. Rather, drugged cats seem to act out their favorite activity—eating, hunting, playing, mating—but this is just acting. Even neutered animals sometimes imitate mating behaviors.

Most experts agree catnip is harmless, but cats may build up a resistance to it. Use catnip sparingly, perhaps as a once or twice-monthly treat. The fresher it is, the better the aroma, and the more your kitty will enjoy it. Cured catnip is available in pet stores, but you may wish to grow your own.

A variety of catnip-stuffed toys are available on the market. Store these in sealed plastic bags to help retain freshness, and they can last three to four years or longer. Be sure to really seal the toy, or kitty will find it—through cupboard doors, boxes, plastic, and all!

© S.E. Livingston

*According to a* Cat Fancy *survey, the top rated commercial toys for cats are "anything with catnip," like this catnip-stuffed mouse.*

## CATNIP

Catnip, catmint, matatabi (silver vine), *Leriana officialis*, and cat thyme all seem to drive kitty wild. The scent turns cats on, acting as a nerve stimulant in the brain, and actually lowering kitty inhibitions and promoting relaxation. Seventy percent of catnip oil is *trans,cis nepetalactone*. It's this chemical that affects cats—even big cats. The molecular structure of trans,cis nepetalactone is similar to that of LSD.

Catnip (*Nepeta cataria*) is a relative of peppermint and spearmint. Catnip sensitivity is a dominant gene that must be inherited; a third of all cats show no reaction at all, and kittens are not affected.

Catnip often causes an initial burst of energy and euphoria; then relaxation hits. Cats will often sniff and lick or chew, shake their heads, rub their face against the catnip (or other objects), and roll—and generally act like engaging, furry fools! Some cats may paw the ground, salivate, or meow incessantly. The effect lasts between five and twenty minutes.

## EATING AND DRINKING

Because they are carnivores, all cats share a similar dental structure. Most felines have thirty teeth at maturity—kittens and cubs have twenty-six. Cat teeth are designed to grasp and cut rather than chew. A cat will turn its head to one side to most effectively use these shearing teeth.

The cat's tongue has rows of hooked, horny, backward-pointing projections (papillae) down its center. The tongue rasps food, and in really big cats, the rough tongue can strip meat from the bones of fallen prey. It also acts as a grooming tool for fur and tones circulation—a kitty tongue gives a great massage. Newborn kittens have only a rim of papillae around the edge of the tongue, which helps grasp the mother's nipple. To drink, a cat curls its tongue backwards, then flicks it forward, rolling it into a spoon shape to scoop liquid. Swallowing occurs every four to five laps.

## DO CATS HAVE TASTE?

Smell and taste are very closely linked. Both senses are registered in the same area of the brain. A cat can taste the same sensations people do—sour, bitter, salty, and sweet—but to a cat, taste isn't nearly as important as smell. It generally doesn't matter to the cat how something tastes, as long as it smells good. A kitty with a stopped-up nose often won't want to eat because it can't smell its food.

A cat's taste buds are located on the edges of the tongue and inside the mouth and lips. Cats experience the strongest taste reaction to sour, which can be detected in all areas. Bitter can be detected only at the back of tongue; salt is at the front. Protein-based chemicals apparently activate kitty taste buds, but animal fats are interpreted as "smells" instead. Although cats can detect sweet, most have only mild interest in the flavor.

Cats remain extremely sensitive to the taste of water; many prefer wet food. The "sandpapery" papillae on the center of the tongue include no taste buds but function instead to collect fluids.

## TOUCH

All cats have sweat glands; because cats are almost totally covered in hair, most of the glands are located in the pads of their feet. You may notice slightly damp paw prints when your cat is hot or frightened.

Paw pads and nose leather are the most sensitive parts of a cat's body. Paws are used to test objects. By tapping the sensitive pad against objects, kitty can determine if it is or is not safe.

Scattered across the cat's fur-covered skin are tiny lumps that act as pressure-sensitive pads. Direct contact isn't required; merely brushing hair adjacent to a pad triggers a response. The guard hairs are more sensitive, while whiskers are the most sensitive of all.

Cats have highly tactile whiskers (vibrissae), set much deeper in the skin than other hair, that transmit messages swiftly to the brain. Scientists haven't fully explained the

*The skin of kitty's neck is five times thicker than on his hind legs, but overall, cats have thinner skin than humans. When human skin contacts feline fur, the result is mutual pleasure.*

whisker function but believe whiskers act something like antennae. They're used to measure openings when a cat enters a narrow space and are also able to "feel" and interpret an incredible amount of additional information. Whiskers protect the eyes—flick a cat's whiskers, and it blinks in reflex. These stiff hairs are also sensitive to air currents and changes of pressure due to close objects.

Cats enjoy and prefer warmth and can tolerate temperatures to about 126 degrees F/52 degrees C before registering pain. Many a cat will snooze on top of a heater that is too hot for us to touch. Because of insensitivity to heat, a cat may not react immediately even if its tail catches fire.

The nose and surrounding skin are the only parts of a cat terribly sensitive to temperature, and here kitty can

If a cat's whiskers are severed, it may lose its equilibrium and stumble into things. Wild felines may even lose their hunting and killing techniques.

detect differences of one to two degrees. Cats prefer their food to be body temperature (about 102 degrees F/38 degrees C), which is why many cats snub food that has been refrigerated.

Touch is a pleasurable sensation that is important emotionally as well. The cat loves to be stroked; this is the first sensation it experiences as a kitten when washed by Mom. When a cat (or human) is stroked, the nervous system responds by slowing the heart rate, tense muscles loosen up as the body relaxes, and the increase of digestive juices and saliva flow may enhance digestion. The opposite reactions occur with fear, or deprivation of touch.

Cats enjoy the sensation of being stroked—probably as much as we humans delight in accommodating them.

In the Middle Ages, a singed cat was worth less than an unmarked kitty. Buyers felt if kitty lay around in front of the fire, it couldn't be a good mouser.

*Kitty's skin is loose for protection, enabling a struggling cat to turn about in its skin and slip from a predator's grasp. This goldfish doesn't have that advantage.*

© Grace Davies/Envision

# CLAWS

A cat's claws are composed of keratin and grow continuously from the last bone of the toe. In a relaxed position, claws are retracted beneath a sheath of skin. When kitty contracts muscles to tighten tendons below the bone, it straightens the toes and extends the claws.

Cats may need nails trimmed to keep them from growing back into the pad. Use very sharp scissors or kitty nail trimmers (guillotine-type). Gently hold the paw and press to expose the claws. The pink "quick" contains nerves and blood vessels that should never be cut. The white tips are like our own fingernails and can be trimmed without pain. Trim no closer than one-eighth (three millimeters) inch from the pink portion.

Cats don't scratch to be vindictive or bad; scratching is instinctive, a way to remove outer sheaths of claws to make room for new growth. Scratching is also good exercise; stretching and digging claws keeps leg, shoulder, and back muscles well toned. It just plain feels good to a cat to scratch, and cats may do it to express happiness or to mark territory.

Unfortunately, some kitties pick furniture or other inappropriate places to scratch. "Punishing instinctive behavior (like scratching) would be like correcting a baby each time it tried to use its hands," say Warren and Fay Eckstein in *How to Get Your Cat to Do What You Want*. Sadly, many cat owners prefer to declaw their cats, rather than deal with this natural behavior more positively.

Declawing consists of amputation of the last joint of each kitty toe. This is a relatively simple surgery, but if it is not done cleanly and correctly, the claw may regrow deformed, putting the cat through much pain and further surgery to correct the situation.

Some cats have one or more extra toes (polydactylism). This is a genetically dominant characteristic passed to offspring. This characteristic makes the cat look like it is wearing mittens.

Many cat organizations protest the practice of declawing and won't allow declawed cats to be shown. A declawed cat is unable to climb or defend against attack. It can't scratch an itch or groom properly, and may experience a change in personality from feeling intimidated. Declawed cats should never be allowed outside, unless on a leash and under supervision.

A more natural alternative is letting kitty keep its claws and providing opportunities to scratch proper objects. A scratching post is "must have" equipment when you first bring kitty home. Starting right will eliminate many behavior problems before they develop.

Most cats know what to do with a scratching post, but if the kitten is young, make like a cat and use the post yourself. The sound will alert kitty to what fun you're having. Place the post in a convenient area near the cat bed or food bowl (cats enjoy a good scratch after eating or sleeping). If the post is stuck away in the corner of an empty room, don't expect the cat to hunt it down; it would rather stay with you and use your footstool!

## KITTY REPELLENT:

Raw onion is extremely unattractive to cats, as is vinegar. Rue (*Ruta graveolens*) is a plant that was used in the first century A.D. to repel the cat, but its oil is so strong it can burn human skin. Check with your veterinarian before using any cat repellent—depending on the purpose, he or she may have much better suggestions.

THE INCOMPARABLE CAT

If kitty already has bad scratching habits, whenever you catch it in the act, firmly say "No!" and take the cat to the post and place (don't force) the paws on it. Praise the cat for scratching proper objects. If you have the right kind of post, kitty should actually prefer it to the soft sofa. In any case, your pet should soon get the idea of what prompts a "No!" and what prompts praise. Be consistent, and always praise.

The best way to prevent a cat from scratching the wrong objects is to give it something better to scratch. The post should be taller than your cat's full-length stretch, with a sturdy base so the cat can't knock it over. The best scratching posts are covered with sisal, which is a rough hemp product, and can usually be found in pet supply stores. A carpet-covered scratching post may be easy to color coordinate with your room, but most cats prefer rough surfaces that give claws resistance (like plaster walls or wooden chair legs) as opposed to anything else.

The Felix Post (made by The Felix Company) is sisal covered and comes in a variety of sizes. Some scratching posts are quite expensive, and they can even be custom-built; do you think your cat would like a personal tree, complete with rough bark and perches? Pet stores are a good place to look, or turn to the back of *Cat Fancy* or *Cats* magazines for addresses of manufacturers.

A less expensive alternative (I promise your cat will never know!) is to make your own. Use old carpet, wrong side out, to cover a wooden post attached to a solid base. Or, cover a piece of plywood, again with carpet wrong side out, and mount against a wall. Try rubbing the post with catnip—a guaranteed turn-on for most cats.

One of the biggest reasons for scratching in the wrong places is boredom, so remember to spark your cat's interest. Rotate the scratching toys and provide choices; you'll have a scratch-happy cat in no time.

"Be careful of this human love, for it can be more painful than being beaten with a stick. People often stop loving and leave one. We never do."

The feline narrator,
from *The Silent Miaow*

© Norvia Behling

# Feline Responsibility

Don Marquis: "what in hell have i done to deserve all these kittens?"

mehitabel

Look at your watch, please. Each hour, three thousand puppies and kittens are born in the United States. Each year, more than twelve million pets are surrendered to animal shelters. It is estimated that four million pregnancies would have to be eliminated to prevent the births of twenty million furry babies destined to someday be surrendered or abandoned.

There's no doubt about it. Kittens are cute, cuddly, and endearing. But cat lovers must be aware of their responsibility to prevent, rather than perpetuate, kitten births. With the growing popularity of cats, it's not surprising that the number of felines in the United States should be growing. However, cat fanciers realize it's not out of love that population is exploding, but rather, ignorance and mismanagement.

With so many throwaway, unloved kittens already available, it's a crime against catdom to breed your kitty—male or female! I can think of no valid excuse to allow any cat to roam and breed. Spayed and neutered pets are better, more affectionate companions. Unaltered animals often have more behavior and temperament problems than spayed or neutered pets.

Neutering males reduces roaming, fighting (and subsequent wound infections), and spraying to mark territory. It also reduces the chance of prostate cancer. Spayed females no longer experience estrus or associated annoying behavior. Spaying eliminates uterine and ovarian cancer and greatly reduces the incidence of breast cancer.

Responsible breeders support altering, and many require kittens be sterilized when they are sold. Cat fanciers generally breed only a very few selected felines that are extraordinary examples of the breed. Even championship cats that have produced fantastic kittens are often spayed or neutered when retired. Harley, a grand champion Abyssinian that has sired over fifteen grand champions will be neutered although he is only four years old because his owners want him to enjoy life as a pet. "Harley will be neutered to improve the quality of his life," say owners Gene and Kitty Rankin.

There are more than enough good, responsible breeders like the Rankins; unfortunately, there are even more irresponsible persons breeding cats. If you can't be discouraged from breeding, at least don't be a fool; find a reputable breeder, and study before you start—find out what you're getting into before embarking. Are you prepared to support all the kittens produced for their lifetimes (fifteen-plus years) if they can't be sold?

Think hard—the very lives of your unborn kitties are at stake.

On average, a cat's litter consists of one to eight kittens, but a four-year-old Burmese needed a cesarean to give birth to nineteen kittens in 1970. Fifteen of the litter survived.

MYTH: "Altered pets get fat and lazy."

TRUTH: Pets get fat and lazy if fed too much without enough exercise.

MYTH: "It's better to have one litter first."

TRUTH: There is no medical evidence that having a litter is good for your pet.

MYTH: "My cat should have kittens; he/she's a purebred."

TRUTH: Twenty-five percent of the pets surrendered to shelters each year are purebred.

MYTH: "I can find homes for the litter."

TRUTH: Those homes won't be available for any of the millions of kittens already born.

MYTH: "I want my children to experience the miracle of birth."

TRUTH: You're actually teaching that kittens are disposable and can be created and discarded as it suits the breeder. Instead, explain that the real miracle is life, and preventing births of some pets saves the lives of others.

If unaltered, one female cat and her offspring can produce, in a seven-year period, 420,000 kittens. Nearly eight million, a staggering four kittens out of every litter of five, are euthanized because there just aren't enough good homes to go around.

The kitten you hold on your lap is the lucky fifth. Before you allow a tragedy to continue, look at your watch.

Please.

# REPRODUCTION

"Far in the distance, a cat languishes loudly."

William Ernest Henley

The queen experiences no pain with the mating. Her screams and postcoital rolling are not fully understood, but may, in some way, induce necessary hormonal changes.

Some females mature very early and experience heat (estrus) by six months or even earlier. Kitty will not be shy about letting the whole world know and will vocalize incessantly, calling for "Tom-of-my-dreams." She will luxuriously roll on the floor, rub against you, the sofa, and everything else in sight, and become extremely affectionate.

In arranged breedings, the female is sent to male. After exploratory sniffing and rubbing, she crouches in front of him with her tail to one side and posterior raised and treads the ground. The male gently grabs the back of her neck with his teeth and straddles her, treading with his own rear paws. He inserts his penis into her vagina, and ejaculation occurs after only a few hard thrusts. She cries out and turns on the male, who dodges if he's smart. A cat's ovaries don't release eggs until after copulation, when the tom's spine-covered penis stimulates ovulation. Eggs aren't released until twenty-four hours after the first mating.

In about three weeks, if the breeding has been successful, the first clear sign will be an enlarging and pinkening of the nipples. Kitty won't be noticeably swollen until about the fifth or sixth week of the pregnancy. Average pregnancy is sixty-five days, and about two weeks before the birth, Mom will start looking for a good place to bear her kittens. Invariably, her choice is inconvenient for human companions. Typically, this is someplace such as your bed pillow or the back of your closet.

The queen will pant and purr and head for her chosen nest during the first stage of labor, which may last six hours. The second stage lasts ten to thirty minutes, but no longer than ninety minutes; during this stage, contractions of the abdomen begin and the mama will bear down to expel the kitten. The third stage is the expulsion of the placenta that accompanies each kitten.

About a third of all kittens are born "backwards," tail first. Usually this is no problem; kittens are very pliable.

## GET HELP!

DURING THE BIRTH: Call the vet if your cat's bearing down produces no kittens after ninety minutes (this behavior should be very obvious—you can see the abdomen clench, and the cat will pant and push and be tensed); if there's a discharge, but no bearing down has been seen; or if labor stops and the queen is still carrying kittens.

AFTER THE BIRTH: Call for help if the queen bleeds from the vulva; has a colored, white, or foul-smelling discharge; is lethargic; doesn't resume normal eating in twelve hours; is abnormally restless or feverish; or shows no interest in her kittens.

# KITTENS

As each kitten is born, the queen breaks the membrane that covers it and licks it to stimulate breathing and circulation. She cuts the cord and often eats the afterbirth. Kittens immediately seek mama's milk; the first milk (colostrum) contains important antibodies and nutrients.

A newborn kitten is four to six inches long and weighs two to five ounces. It has a flat face, its eyes are closed, its ears are folded back, and it can barely move. By the second to third day, each kitten claims its "own" teat by smell and nurses from it exclusively.

The kitten's eyes open at between eight and twenty days. All kittens start out with blue eyes. Crawling begins about the sixteenth day, and at three weeks, kittens begin using paws to pat things that interest them.

If a kitten is very cold and weak, dunk it up to its neck in a bowl of 101°F (38 °C) water (kitten body temperature) for two to three minutes, and stroke and massage it until it becomes more active. Dry with warm towels. Canned queen's milk is fed to orphan kittens or used for supplemental feedings. Tiny kittens must be fed every two hours. After every feeding, rub the kitten's stomach and anal opening to stimulate passage of waste.

*Kittens will play with anything. A kitten deprived of play may suffer emotionally later, develop learning disabilities, or have a lower IQ.*

*Scottish Fold Kittens*

THE PHYSICAL CAT
79

Most cats favor one paw or the other. Twenty percent are left-pawed, forty percent right-pawed, and the rest ambidextrous.

Mom will begin weaning around twenty-one days. By this age, kittens naturally imitate her and can be trained to drink milk from a bowl. They also begin to play and learn the fine art of washing. This is the time Mom begins toilet training, and by watching her, kittens learn to bury their waste.

At four weeks, kittens begin to demand food, rather than waiting for Mom to ring the dinner bell. By age six to eight weeks, they will be ready to leave Mom.

## PLAY

A kitten's brain is almost fully mature at five weeks and has the sensory capability of an adult, but motor development takes longer. Play helps develop motor skills and prepares kittens for life. From four weeks old on, kittens practice technique.

Four basic actions are learned in play: play fighting, mouse pounce, bird swat, and fish scoop. The first play displayed by kittens is on the back, belly-up, with paws waving. Feints at the back of a sibling's neck mock the prey-bite used later to hunt and dispatch mice. Kittens also practice the simpering sideways walk, back arched high, almost tiptoeing around other kittens or objects. Soon, coordination improves to execute the pounce; the

"When I play with my cat, who knows if I am not a pastime to her more than she is to me?"

Michel Eyquem de Montaigne

boxer stance; chase and pursuit; horizontal leaps; and, a favorite, the face-off—where kittens enthusiastically bat each other about the head.

## CAT TOYS

The absolute worst toy for your cat is your own hand and fingers. This may be cute when kitty is tiny, but a big tom cat bite down on tender fingers. Instead, give kitty something it can really sink teeth and claws into, without accidentally drawing blood.

Cat-proof your toys. Regulators watch for dangerous children's toys, but there's no one but you to look out for your cat. The string attached to play mice can be swallowed; plastic eyes and other pieces are equally dangerous. If kitty must have such a toy, pull off removable parts first. Always supervise even the innocuous ball of yarn, which can be deadly if ingested. **Keep kitty away from the sewing basket and thread;** a needle is easily swallowed and requires surgical removal.

The ideal cat toy is very light, easily moved with a casual paw swipe, and soft for teeth and claws to grip. The problem with most toys is they just lie there. After the initial thrill wears off, kitty may lose interest. To titillate your cat, give the toy preylike motion by pulling and pushing it. But remember, it will frustrate your cat if you don't play fair and let it actually catch the prey once in a while.

The all-time favorite cat toy is the Kitty Tease by Galkie Company. It is also an excellent means of exercise to keep your cat in shape, or to slim down a rotund tabby. Kitty Tease is like a flexible fishing pole with a lure of denim strips at the end of a durable line. Kitty will go absolutely wild, turning somersaults, leaping and stalking, as you make it dance beyond her reach or sweep it across the floor just out of range. Remember always to put the Kitty Tease away, or your in-house lion will destroy it.

Cat Dancer is another excellent toy, composed of a wire with tight rolls of paper on each end. It bounces and hops unpredictably and will give your cat many hours of exercise and delight. Look in pet stores, or in *Cat Fancy* and *Cats* magazines for these and other wonderful cat toys.

© Norvia Behling

## CHEAP THRILLS

Many cats and kittens create their own entertainment. A paper bag placed on its side makes a great playground for the inventive cat—hide-and-seek, all alone! Ping-Pong balls are light enough for kitty to toss around. Try putting one inside an empty tissue box, and enjoy kitty's antics "fishing" for it. Peacock feathers are also fun, but an unsupervised cat may eat the feather, so be sure to put it away when playtime is over. The cardboard roll from the toilet paper is also loads of fun, and aluminum foil balls are shiny and make an interesting noise, as do crumpled up balls of paper. Use your imagination; it will keep the kitten in your cat.

© S.E. Livingston

*A Cat Fancy survey reports that the number one non-commercial cat toy kitties preferred was the plastic ring from the milk jug. Cats often find their own household favorites, but you should always supervise to be sure it's a cat-safe choice.*

*Does kitty know the difference between your old armchair and the brand-new sofa? If allowed on one, kitty is sure to think all furniture is fair game.*

# Rules of the House

Cats aren't stupid—if anything, they're too smart. Cats know that by acting independent, most people won't expect them to obey, and they'll be left alone. Don't let kitty pick what she wants to do. And talk, talk, TALK to your cat. Cats have the ability to learn a large human vocabulary, and the more kitty understands of your language, the fewer misunderstandings and behavioral problems there will be.

Teach your kitten very early the meaning of a solid, authoritative "No!" This should be all that's necessary to correct poor behavior. Never slap or hit your cat, or it will associate your hands with punishment. Punishing your cat "after the fact" has no effect; kitty won't understand the connection between the chair she scratched three hours ago and your anger now. Chasing kitty after scolding will make it afraid of you. Cats become embarrassed very easily (they show this by nervous grooming). Let kitty run and hide and lick its hurt pride in private.

Don't dwell exclusively on negatives, or kitty will realize it gets more attention when it does something wrong. Encourage good behavior. Praise the dickens out of your cat when it does something right—when it plops in the litter pan or scratches the cat tree instead of the new sofa.

Consistency is key. Don't let your cat get away with something one time and correct it another—it will just get confused. Besides, it isn't fair when you change the rules.

# CAT LANGUAGE

Do you speak cat? Felinese is not easy to master; cats communicate with body posture, tail and ear positions and movements, and even the angle of the body in relation to other objects or animals. Cats also respond to verbal cues and scent.

Although we aren't equipped to interpret the finer points, most cat lovers understand a lot more than they think.

A cat's mood can be read by how dilated or narrow the slit of the pupil is and by the position of eyelids. Sudden dilation of the eyes indicates strong emotional arousal. This may be caused by sudden fright, or something as mundane as a hungry cat being presented with a bowl of favorite food.

Slit-eyes indicate aggression, as does unblinking staring. If you notice dilated pupils suddenly contract to a slit, it may be kitty has had enough of the toddler and is preparing to strike! Cats with wide-open eyes are generally on the alert; they don't want to miss a thing. Avoid locking eyes with kitty — even though you're merely admiring the cat, it will interpret your interest as threatening. Half-closed eyes (the sleepy-eyed look) indicates relaxation and trust. Closed eyes are a sure bet kitty is taking a catnap.

Cats also signal mood with their tails. A vertical tail signifies friendly approach. Kittens run to mother, and cats greet owners, with this tail display. When it curves down and up, kitty is usually content and peaceful; a slightly curved and raised tail shows interest, a lowered fluffed tail shows fear. If the tail is quiet with only the tip twitching, kitty is irritated; expect a swipe from a paw! A cat that wags its tail violently from side to side is usually angry and about to attack.

Fluffed fur indicates excitement of some kind (fear, threat, arousal, play). Bristled fur on a straight tail means aggression, but a tail arched and bristled shows defensive-

© Greg Crisci/Photo/Nats

*An alert cat*

**ALERT**
*eyes and ears forward, moderate eye dilation*

**OFFENSIVE**
*ears to side, eyes evasive, slight dilation*

**DEFENSIVE**
*ears flat, eyes fully dilated, snarl display*

**AFRAID**
*ears to side and pressed down, eyes fully dilated, narrowed eyelids, lip-teeth display*

## DID YOU SAY "MEOW?"

Experts have identified sixteen different kitty voice patterns classified under four groups: murmur patterns, such as purring and trilling, occur when kitty is in a friendly relaxed state; vowel patterns, like meowing, are used to gain attention; articulated sounds, or chittering, are generally associated with solicitation and frustration; strained intensity sounds, like hissing, growling, and screaming, are used primarily to attack or defend, and in mating.

A *Cat Fancy* survey reported that ninety seven percent of its readers feed dry cat food, while canned varieties were a close second.

ness; the cat may attack if further provoked. Relaxed happy cats keep whiskers extended in the mouth area; if bristly, or pulled back tight along the face, aggression, or fear with the possibility of aggression is the translation.

Body position also offers clues. A confident cat will threaten head on, with a direct stare and a body poised to rush and strike. An apprehensive cat arches its back sideways to the adversary, in order to look bigger and more impressive. Submission or surrender is indicated by crouching, with ears down, tail tucked, and all four feet under the body.

## FEEDING THE CAT

Scarf, snarf, gobble, slurp, gulp, scrounge. No matter how you say it, eating is one of life's oldest, dearest pleasures—according to our cats, that is. Does dinnertime mean confrontation with Morris' Evil Twin? Or is your cat victim to the Garfield Syndrome, a finicky eater that wants only what's on your plate? Does kitty eat to live, or live to eat?

Cats are true carnivores; their intestines, being designed purely for meat digestion, are proportionally shorter than humans'. You'll discover kitty loves poultry, fish, eggs, and meat, but a commercial diet will provide a better balance and be easier to prepare. Cats require four times more protein than dogs. Don't feed kitty dog food, or vice versa, or serious problems could result.

NEVER FEED YOUR CAT TUNA! Tuna is high in polyunsaturated fat, which cats have trouble metabolizing. Tuna can rob a cat's body of vitamin E, leading to a painful disease called steatitis, or Yellow Fat Disease, in which the skin becomes unbearably tender.

Cats also love milk, yogurt, ice cream, cheese—almost any milk product. However, adult cats have difficulty digesting milk sugar, and diarrhea is often the result of milk fed to weaned kittens or adult cats. Small amounts as a treat are okay if diarrhea is not a problem, but milk should never take the place of water. Cats should be encouraged to drink as much water as possible, to help prevent urinary disorders.

Is your cat like Garfield, who would subsist on munchies alone if given a choice? Cats enjoy a variety of people foods. Olives affect some cats like catnip, while other kitties prefer chips and snacks. Eating grass is common and not unhealthy, for it contains vitamins and acts as a natural emetic. Cats also like tomato sauce, and don't be

© Domenico Ruzzo/Envision

surprised if kitty begs for fruits and vegetables. Melon and corn on the cob are generally favorites.

Diane Gergel's cat has the ideal strategy. "Putter opens the refrigerator," she says; "and helps himself. He uses his nose to break the magnetic lock and pushes the door open. To keep him out, we had to put a bungee cord on the refrigerator door."

Many cats are creatures of habit that want their bowls to be consistently in the same place. Other cats could care less about location, as long as the bowl is full of food. Some kitties prefer privacy and quiet for dining, while a few enjoy the friendly competition of communal feeding.

Chocolate is toxic to cats— beware of Easter Bunnies!

Tracy Jacobi's cat Miffi insists on eating on the dining room table so the other cat can't reach her bowl. Another cat named Dusty only drinks from her water bowl if it's perched on top of the aquarium. Nicole Beaumont says, "Serendipity requiries the presence of my two gerbils, the absence of our golden retriever and the family, and three food and water dishes in a row where they always are." And Amie Harris' cat Daniel is so particular, "He'll move the bowl with his paw until it's in the right place." Every cat will require something just a little bit different.

Bowl type is another important factor in dining. Bowls should be heavy enough that they don't tip over or make

Common houseplants can be deadly: Philodendron, dumb cane (Dieffenbachia), elephant's-ear (Caladium), poinsettia, rhododendron, azalea, and mistletoe, among others, are poisonous. Monitor kitty's grazing!

*Warming food in the microwave will often appeal to the finicky cat's taste. Some cat owners have been successful by spiking snubbed food with brewer's yeast or catnip.*

kitty "follow" them around the room. Long-haired and flat-faced cats need shallower dishes to keep from dirtying themselves when they eat. The bowl must be comfortable for your cat, with plenty of whisker-room—cats dislike crumpled whiskers. Some cats are allergic to plastic dishes, which are also harder to clean than other types. Ceramic dishes are excellent, but should be made in the United States to ensure the glaze is lead-free and safe. Glass doesn't hold odors, but be careful with chips or cracks. Stainless steel is tops—nearly indestructible, easy to clean, and chip-resistant—my favorite!

*How* cats eat is as entertaining and varied as *what* they eat. Some refuse food that falls out of the bowl; others purposely carry bits to the living room rug before munching down. Some cats, like Karen Commings', utilize "kitty utensils" to dine. "Dusty lifts food and water into her mouth using her front paws. If she gets food to her mouth and decides she doesn't really want it, she flings it across the room. I spend a lot of time cleaning little kitty meatballs off the floor."

Every cat has its own eccentricities. We've all known people whose life revolves around food; cats aren't so different, if you think about it. Anita Jacobs' cat Runt-mo "will do *anything* to get to food. He dove for a potato chip once, and bit my lip along with the chip! Runt-mo has a real eating disorder."

I guess that depends on who's holding the munchies.

Toxoplasmosis is caused by a protozoan parasite that may spread through egg spores in cat feces. The disease is dangerous to unborn babies, and pregnant women should avoid cleaning litter. Since egg spores must incubate several days to spread disease, regular daily cleaning is the best prevention.

## BATHROOM ETIQUETTE

Probably the least pleasant element of living with cats is dealing with kitty's "litter-ary" needs. Cats are by nature extremely fastidious, clean animals. They won't eliminate where they eat, sleep, or play, and they bury their waste. In the wild, this behavior keeps odor from attracting predators to the den.

It's rarely necessary to train a kitten to use the litter box; usually, a kitten will follow Mom to the litter pan, dig around, smell, and soon know what to do. For the occasional kitten that needs a little extra help, show it where the box is (right after a meal is best) and scratch the litter with your finger or with kitty's front paw. Usually, kittens get the idea very quickly. Praise the dickens out of kitty when a proper deposit is made. Monitoring the box helps with early diagnosis of health problems, too.

Placement of kitty's toilet is very important. It must be convenient for the cat to use, but not too close to eating or sleeping areas to offend the fastidious cat nature. Some cats are very shy and private when it comes to toilet habits, so make sure the litter pan is placed in a private area. Attractive folding screens are available, or covered boxes do the trick.

Standard litter pans, made of easily cleaned plastic, are about twelve by eighteen inches. Larger pans are available and often work better for bigger or standing-pose cats that tend to miss smaller models. There's a huge variety of pans available in pet stores and mail-order catalogs, but some cat owners prefer making their own from cardboard boxes, baby bathtubs, or dishpans. Some commercial pans come with hoods for kitty privacy, which also cuts down odor. Covers also help with enthusiastic diggers that kick litter out of the box or those that tend to hang over the edge and miss the target.

Some cats don't like to share potties; in these instances, you'll need one for each cat. Others will share, and a single giant-size pan may suffice. Keep a small whisk broom and pan handy to clean up litter tracking, and "near misses." Plastic litter-pan liners are excellent in theory; you lift the whole mess out for convenient cleaning. In reality, cat claws and plastic rarely mix successfully.

Clay litter is more absorbent and less messy than cedar chips, sawdust, or sand. Some new litters are designed to be flushable, which is very convenient. Others absorb liquid waste into easily removed solid balls, which prolongs the life of the litter. Although deodorized litter smells better to humans, it unfortunately often offends the cat's sensitive nose.

B oodabox and Kitti-Potti receive thumbs up from many cat people. Boodabox is very sturdy so it doesn't knock over, and it has a replaceable charcoal filter in the lid to cut down on odor. Both boxes are covered and can be found in most pet stores; ordering information is also in *Cat Fancy* magazine.

© J. Bisley/Unicorn Stock Photos

B etter Way Litter, made by Sanex Corporation, and Ever Clean Cat Litter, by A & M Pet Products Inc., both of Houston, Texas, received raves from survey respondents in *Cat Fancy* magazine. These litters allow liquid waste to be removed when it congeals in balls, keeping litter fresher longer.

By staying on top of cleaning, you can easily control most odors. Baking soda sprinkled in the litter helps absorb odors. Deodorant powders and sprays may be helpful, but wait until kitty isn't around—the initial smell may be offensive, and the spray may be terrifying. About a two-inch layer of litter is best. Once you find a litter that works well and kitty likes, don't change brands unless necessary. Don't make the litter experience bad, or your cat will look for a better place to potty.

> Changes in diet can help reduce both bulk and odor of solid wastes. Iams and Hill's Science Diet Feline Maintenance are excellent products.

Use a slotted spatula or kitty scoop for daily removal of fecal matter; this will lengthen the life of litter because kitty won't reject the full box. Thoroughly clean the pan and change the litter every few days as needed—sometimes weekly is enough, but oftener may be better. Remember to thoroughly rinse away the odor of the cleanser, or kitty may avoid the bathroom—such sensitive noses!

At about six to nine months of age, unaltered male cats begin to use urine to mark territory. They back up into position, their tail (held vertically) slightly trembles, and they spray urine over the object. Cats won't mark over another's mark, unlike dogs, who pee on everything.

© Norvia Behling

## HIT OR MISS?

A *Cat Fancy* survey reported that most cats' potty habits are above reproach; seventy-nine percent never urinate outside the box, seventy-six percent never defecate inappropriately, and sixty-two percent claim perfect scores. That still leaves twenty to forty percent that *occasionally* perform an OOPS. Don't be surprised if your kitty is one of these.

Cats "go" in the wrong places for any number of reasons: not wanting to "share" with another cat, stress, change in family (new baby, marriage, divorce, new pet, loss of pet), dirty box, litter pan too small (perhaps the cover is uncomfortable for a tall cat to squat comfortably), pan smells wrong, litter too dusty, etc. Some cats have the best of intentions, but their aim is off. Most importantly, cats break training when they're sick. Whenever an accident occurs, be sure you know *why,* so you can act appropriately to prevent recurrence.

Once kitty starts using a corner of the room, it's hard to break the habit. Clean "accidents" with vinegar and water, or use a commercial odor neutralizer to discourage a repeat accident (Nature's Miracle is a good brand). If kitty continues to use the spot, discourage it with aluminum foil laid over those areas, or an upside-down plastic carpet protector (with the little nibs up).

Hard-case cats that habitually leave little presents around the house can be dissuaded by feeding them in those places. Divide normal dinner portions onto paper plates and set them in the notorious spots. Since kitty will avoid voiding where it eats, this should do the trick. Once the cat is broken of the old habit, return to the old feeding spot.

# CAT CARE

The best way to choose a veterinarian is to seek recommendations from other cat owners. All vets will do their best for your kitty, but one doctor's temperament may suit your cat (and you) better than another. Charges vary, so you may wish to shop around. More importantly, choose a veterinarian you can trust. After all, you're dealing with your cat's health.

VETERINARY MEDICINE IS CONSTANTLY IMPROVING, AND INFORMATION QUICKLY BECOMES OBSOLETE. THE FOLLOWING MATERIAL IS MEANT ONLY AS A GUIDE; CONSULT YOUR VETERINARIAN FOR THE MOST CURRENT INFORMATION.

© Norvia Behling

## ROUTINE VACCINATIONS

Your cat should receive an exam and vaccinations as soon as you get it. To be fully protected, kittens (just like human babies) need a series of booster shots two weeks apart; the first should be given at age six to eight weeks. Once the series has been completed, yearly vaccinations protect adult cats thereafter.

Feline *rhinotracheitis* and *calicivirus* cause upper respiratory disease in cats, which includes coldlike symptoms (watering eyes and nose) and can develop into pneumonia. *Feline pneumonitis* also causes purulent eye and nasal discharge, with sneezing. *Feline panleukopenia* (distemper) produces depression, fever, diarrhea, and vomiting, and has a ninety percent mortality rate. *Rabies* acts on the nervous system and results in paralysis and death. *Feline leukemia* causes a variety of diseases and symptoms, including cancers and immune suppression that make cats prone to other illnesses. *Feline infectious peritonitis* (FIP) also affects the cat's immune system. These diseases are devastating, extremely contagious, and completely preventable with proper vaccinations.

## ALTERING YOUR CAT

Although cats are often sterilized between six to nine months of age, early spay/neuter programs are available that provide the service as early as eight weeks old. In any case, kitty is completely anesthetized and feels no discomfort during surgery. Some cats may be sore for a day or two afterwards while some may experience little or no discomfort.

An *ovariohysterectomy* removes both the ovaries and uterus from inside the lower abdomen of the female cat. A small incision is made on her shaved and sterilized tummy, and the Y-shaped organs are tied off and detached. Stitches closing the tummy are removed in 7-10 days.

*Neutering* is external, and less involved than the spay surgery. After the hair is eliminated, tiny incisions are made in the male's sterilized scrotal sac. The testicles are expressed, drawn out, and removed.

Sterilization is often a requirement of shelter adoptions, and many agencies provide certificates for reduced-cost surgeries that most veterinarians gladly honor. Check with your local agencies today.

# COMMON PARASITES

The *ear mite* lives on the surface of the skin of the ear and feeds by piercing the skin and sucking lymph. Irritation, inflammation, and black, tarry exudate form inside the ear, making kitty scratch and shake its head. *Mange* is caused by a burrowing skin mite and usually results in itchy lesions on the head and neck. Both kinds of mites are extremely contagious and can be eliminated with proper veterinary treatment.

*Ticks* are bloodsucking parasites that attach to skin like tiny balloons. They not only cause painful lesions; ticks also carry disease.

The *flea* is a highly specialized bloodsucking parasite and the number one complaint of pet owners: one cat can house up to two hundred of the wee beasties. Fleas can cause anemia and allergic reactions (scratching), and transmit disease and tapeworms. Both ticks and fleas can be controlled with insecticides.

Cats are extremely sensitive to chemicals, so be very careful with insecticides. Use a veterinary-approved cat-safe product, and treat the house, yard, and your cat by following veterinary and product recommendations.

Cats groom away as many as fifty percent of the fleas covering their bodies, and over forty percent of flea-infested cats have *tapeworms* from swallowing infected fleas.

Cats also get tapeworms from eating rabbits or rodents, but flea control is the best method to prevent most tapeworm infestation and recurrence. Tapeworm segments look like dried grains of rice that stick to the anal area of your cat's fur. An effective and safe drug is available from veterinarians to eliminate the pest.

Other intestinal parasites affecting cats include *hookworms,* which suck blood and can be contracted by eating contaminated food. Weight loss and anemia may result. *Roundworms* live in the stomach or intestines and they look like strings of spaghetti when passed in the stool. Kittens often become infected by swallowing eggs from mother's fur or her milk. In large numbers, they can cause intestinal damage and prevent food digestion. *Threadworms* and *whipworms* are also common parasites. Intestinal worms can be easily eliminated by proper veterinary treatment.

*Heartworms* are a blood parasite transmitted by mosquitoes from animal to animal. They enter the bloodstream as larvae, mature and lodge in the right ventricle or pulmonary artery, and interfere with heart action and blood circulation. Untreated heartworms are fatal. Ask your veterinarian about prevention.

*Haemobartonella* is a protozoan parasite causing feline infectious anemia. It damages red blood cells and causes severe and sometimes fatal anemia. Transmission is probably through flea and tick bites.

# POISON!

Signs of poisoning vary but may include abdominal pain, diarrhea or vomiting, incoordination or convulsions, or difficulty breathing. Household cleaning products, houseplants, and many insecticides can be dangerous. Antifreeze is deadly; it tastes sweet and causes renal damage and death if not treated in time. If you suspect kitty has been poisoned, call a cat poison control center and your veterinarian for instructions on specific action.

© Norvia Behling

# GROOMING

Grooming removes dead hair and loose dander, reduces shedding, and stimulates and distributes natural oils. Cats love the grooming experience—they get scratched and rubbed and massaged in all their favorite places. If fur is matted or tangled, have a professional groomer show you how to keep the coat in good shape. *Hair balls* naturally occur when a cat grooms itself and swallows fur; the hair is either vomited or subsequently passed by defecation. Regular grooming alleviates the problem, and cat laxatives are available to help with elimination. Most cats find hair-ball medication very palatable. Petroleum jelly will also help them pass furballs; kitties often lick off jelly spread on their paws—they love it, and it works as well as many commercial products.

## SPECIAL CONCERNS

Because a cat's skin heals extremely quickly, *abscesses* often occur when the surface heals, but the deeper wound remains. Most abscesses must be surgically drained and treated by a veterinarian. An abscess looks like a fluctuating tender lump beneath the fur, and it is usually located in the cheek/neck area. It can swell to mammoth proportions if not treated. Rupture results in the thickened, scarred jowls and cheeks often found in unaltered toms. Abscesses are painful, and the subsequent infection gives rise to high fevers. Preventing cat fights is the best way to avoid wound abscesses; usually, neutering eliminates the urge to squabble.

*Acne* usually occurs on the chin, when hair follicles become blocked. If at the base of the tail, the condition is called *Stud Tail*. Although Stud Tail affects both sexes, it seems more common in sexually active male Persians and Siamese.

*Diabetes mellitus* results when the pancreas fails to produce enough insulin to move glucose into the cells of the body—kitty can't metabolize food. Symptoms include excessive drinking, excessive urination, increased appetite, and weight loss.

Obesity is often a culprit. Large volumes of fat in an obese cat's body can alter and suppress production of insulin, which results in a diabetic state. This means that very often a cat becomes diabetic as a direct result of being fat. Sometimes, if the cat returns to normal weight, the diabetic state is reversed.

When insulin is unavailable to move glucose into the cells of the body, the body can't use food. Even a well-fed cat with an insulin insufficiency will lose weight, because it may as well be eating sawdust for all the good the food does it.

Eventually, the body turns to other food sources. This can result in a condition known as catabolism. Instead of

*Grooming your cat offers the best opportunity to check out all the little things that might otherwise be overlooked: are her ears clean? do her nails need trimming? are her teeth clean? are her eyes and nose free of discharge?*

metabolizing external nutritional sources, the diabetic animal actually cannibalizes its own fat and muscle tissue, resulting in a dramatic loss of weight. Animals that have progressed to catabolism can rarely be saved.

Treatments include insulin injections and dietary management; however, results on promising research into an oral insulin medication for cats is pending.

When your cat's electrical impulses in the brain go "haywire," they short-circuit normal brain processes, and seizures may result. *Epilepsy* is a common clinical problem requiring ongoing medical management in small animals.

*Feline infectious peritonitis* (FIP) has no known cure, but a new vaccine to prevent the disease is now available. Initial signs are fever, lethargy and loss of appetite. These progress to either a buildup of fluid in the abdomen or variable nervous signs. Euthanasia is usually recommended.

*Lower urinary tract disease* (LUTD) formerly called *feline urologic syndrome* (FUS) is a combination of diseases. It is characterized by the presence of crystals and excessive mucus in the urine. Cats are prone to urologic disorders because many normally urinate only once a day, and some only once every two or three days. The crystals thus have more time to develop.

LUTD affects male, female, neutered, and spayed cats with equal frequency. Crystals in the urine of many affected cats have been linked to dietary magnesium levels, also referred to as ash. Conscientious owners must be aware that ash consists of all non-combustible materials, only one of which is magnesium. Ash may contain primarily salt, or any number of other minerals. Depending on the specific content of "ash" in a given food, it may or may not be beneficial to the cat. Most commercial cat foods are within safe magnesium limits.

© Norvia Behling

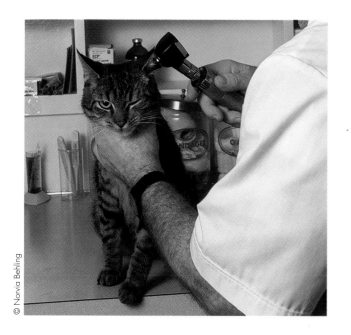
© Norvia Behling

## LUTD WARNING SIGNS

1. A housebroken animal dribbling urine or urinating in unusual locations
2. Frequent voiding of small quantities of urine
3. Bloody urine
4. Urine with a strong ammonia odor
5. Squatting or straining at the end of urination
6. Listlessness and poor appetite and/or excessive thirst

Obstruction from crystals happens oftener in males and is an emergency. **Coma and death occur in 72 hours following complete obstruction.** Treatment eliminates crystals and prevents development of new ones. A prescription diet, such as Hill's C/D, is considered the treatment of choice.

Stress, infectious disease, injury, and bodily dysfunctions cause ill health; pain, fever, and behaviorial changes are the earliest signs. Call your veterinarian any time you suspect kitty is not well—better a false alarm than a dead cat. The best way to recognize illness is to be familiar with well behavior.

## DIAGNOSING THE SICK CAT

A cat's normal temperature ranges from 101 to 102.5 degrees. To take kitty's temperature, get help to gently restrain your cat—it won't like this at all. If you're alone, gently wrap the cat in a blanket or towel to safely restrain it. Grease a rectal thermometer with mineral oil or vaseline, and insert no further than three quarters of an inch. Leave in place for about one minute before reading.

Take a cat's pulse by placing fingers on the chest just behind and level with the cat's elbow. Normal heart rate is 110 to 140 beats a minute; illness or severe stress may induce rates of 300 or more.

© Marty Youngmann

© Christopher Bain

## GERIATRIC MEDICAL CONCERNS

"Nothing's more playful than a young cat, or more grave than an old one."

Thomas Fuller

As health care for our feline friends steadily improves, pet cats are living longer, healthier lives. Today, many cats live well into their mid-twenties, while some have been reported to live as long as thirty-six years. Because the cat's life expectancy has increased, "old cat" problems are a growing concern.

A tabby cat from Devon, England, was put to sleep at the age of thirty-four. Another tabby from Devon celebrated its thirty-sixth birthday on November 28, 1939, and then died the next day. What is it with longevity and Devon, anyway?

### EMERGENCY!

*Asphyxiation* can be caused by smoke inhalation, choking, strangulation, drowning, or electrocution. Whenever a cat stops breathing, time is of the essence. In life-or-death instances of drowning or choking, if the obstruction is not easily removable, grasp kitty by the hind legs, and swing; centrifugal force helps dislodge any blockage. Don't be shy, and use energy.

If this doesn't work, use artificial respiration. Place a palm over the cat's chest immediately behind its elbow, with your other palm on top; press firmly, then quickly release. Repeat every five seconds. Mouth-to-nose respiration may also work. First clear the cat's mouth and throat; then close the mouth, place your lips over his nose, and gently blow. Repeat every two to three seconds.

*Arthritis* occurs most commonly in the elderly pet, just like in people. Affected cats are reluctant to move. They often "favor" the affected limb. Pain is made worse by cold, sudden changes in the weather, or heavy exercise. There is no cure.

WARNING! Tylenol and aspirin given without veterinary supervision can kill your cat; kitty's system can't break down the substance, and even small doses may be deadly.

*Dilated cardiomyopathy* is a fatal heart disease often caused by lack of taurine in the diet. Most manufacturers currently provide adequate taurine in cat food, and the disease has decreased in frequency.

Nearly fifty percent of major heart problems in cats are due to untreated hyperthyroidism. *Hyperthyroidism* occurs when the thyroid gland secretes excessive thyroid hormones, which results in an increased metabolic rate. Hyperthyroidism occurs most commonly in the middle-aged to old cat. The cat loses weight but stays hungry and may develop an oily hair coat. The owner often notices diarrhea, hyperactivity, and/or increased water intake and urination.

The feline *immunodeficiency virus,* FIV or FAIDS, was isolated in 1987 and is similar to the human AIDS virus. Older cats are most often affected, with male cats twice as likely to become infected as female cats. Free-roaming cats are at much higher risk than cats kept indoors. No prevention, treatment, or cure is currently available.

*Lymphosarcoma* is the most frequently diagnosed cancer of cats, with cancer of abdominal organs typical in older animals. Mammary gland carcinoma commonly affects older intact female cats; chances of this developing can be nearly eliminated by spaying before her first heat cycle. Skin tumors and oral tumors are just as dangerous. Any tumor a cat has is more often cancerous than benign. If you find a lump or bump, DON'T WAIT! See your vet immediately.

*Periodontal disease* is a significant problem in middle-aged and older cats. Cats get cavities below the gum line rather than in the tooth crown; the pain will cause them to stop eating, to salivate, and to show much distress. Use a soft, damp cloth over your finger and massage and clean kitty's teeth weekly, or even more frequently, for healthy teeth and gums—if your cat lets you. Start when it is a kitten and make this a part of its grooming regime. (A human baby toothbrush also works well.) Annual cleaning by your vet is recommended.

Although elderly cats must live with infirmities of age to some extent, preventative maintenance in young to middle-aged cats can make them more comfortable. By preventing problems that occur during the senior years, we often prolong a beloved friend's life.

# EUTHANASIA

Cats are born; cats live; cats die. Some die tragically in accidents; some slip away easily in quiet old age; others linger with illness, on and on, and in pain. These last deserve our greatest love.

When injury or illness places kitty in prolonged distress with little hope of recovery; when kitty gives up and longs for release; when selfishly prolonging life means but additional pain for the cat—these are situations that may call for euthanasia, a determination that only you, as best friend, can make.

Euthanasia is painless, consisting of a single needle prick followed by one last quiet breath. Most veterinarians agree to your being with the cat, to offer comfort as it passes on. You loved your cat best—only you will know when the time is right to end the suffering. Have faith in your decision, for it is the finest final gift you can give.

Then after a time, celebrate your cat's life—not by replacing it, but by remembering, with another of its kind. Other cats need you, and such unselfish love should not be wasted.

## CHAPTER FOUR

# Choosing Your Cat

D ecisions, decisions: kitten or adult? Long-haired or shorthaired? Purebred or alley? Kittens are awfully cute, and purebreds offer exotic looks and an anticipated personality. But adults are more settled, and mutt cats are endearing, healthy, more needy—and usually free.

Whatever you decide, a healthy cat is best. Fur should be glossy, eyes should be bright with interest, and eyes, ears, and nose should be free of gummy deposits or discharge. Check kitty's bottom for signs of diarrhea or tapeworm segments. The belly should be rubbery, not hard or flabby.

Temperament is just as important as health. The cat should not be timid, but willing to make friends; a kitten

# Gallery of Breeds

*Opposite page: Russian*
*Blue*

Hold up the tail to determine the sex of a kitten. A girl kitten's anus and vulva will look like a semicolon; boy cat's bottom looks more like an exclamation point.

ought to be ready to play, and ready to forgive loud, sudden noises and be coaxed back to you. A cat that fails these tests may remain aloof around people its whole life.

Always support the body; don't let kitty dangle from the armpits. Lift a cat with one hand beneath the chest just behind the front legs, and the other cupping the posterior.

When introducing a second cat, include new litter pans, bowls, and toys for New Cat to reduce Old Cat's irritation. Most kitties are cranky until reassured that their place in your affections hasn't been usurped. Have someone else deliver New Cat, so Old Cat won't blame you—and let the cats meet initially only through the carrier. During introductions, don't pet New Cat; it will be distracted enough, and you mustn't ruffle Old Cat's fur. Until they become friends, separate the cats when you leave the house. Some friendships are immediate, but others take time, so be patient.

The first recorded cat show was at St. Giles Fair in Winchester, England, in 1958. The first National Cat Club was formed in 1887 in Britain, with Harrison Weir as the first president.

*Persian*

## CAT TYPES

Cobby (Persian) type is solidly built with short, thick legs, broad shoulders and rump, and short, rounded head with flat face, and almost round eyes.

Domestic (American Shorthair) has a chunky body, medium-length legs, average shoulders and rump, short neck, medium-length rounded head, and almond or round eyes. It is very muscular.

Foreign (Siamese) is a lithe, lightly built cat with long slim legs, narrow shoulders and rump, and long, narrow wedge-shaped head with widely spread and sometimes slanted eyes. Ears are more pointed than the domestic's. Although it looks fragile, the foreign is as sturdy as the domestic.

Cat breeds come in an amazing variety of shapes, sizes, colors, and patterns. Registering associations demand standards for each breed; however, standards vary from one association to another, and breeds accepted in one may not be recognized by others.

# COAT TYPES

Cats have four types of coats: down is the soft undercoat that keeps kitty warm; awn are the middle hairs that insulate and guard skin; guard hairs are the longest and thickest and provide a protective outer coat; vibrissae are the whiskers.

"Tabby" is derived from the cat's resemblance to the markings on black-and-white watered silks, which originated from El Tabbiana, near Bagdad.

Colors include white, black, blue (shades of gray), chocolate, cinnamon; lilac/lavender (very light gray), fawn, red, cream, ruddy, sorrel, champagne, platinum, mink, caramel, beige, apricot, indigo, and silver (tipped/smoked cats).

*Left: Oriental Blue,*
*Above: Long-haired Cat*
*Below: Calico Maine Coon*

Patterns include agouti (bands of ticking on each individual hair); tabby (spotted, classic/marbled, and mackerel/striped); bicolor; tortoiseshell (mixture of red and black); tricolor; tipped (light hair with dark tip, or dark with light tip); and point (light body with darker "points"—face, lower legs, tail).

THE INCOMPARABLE CAT

*Grey Persian*

In the next section, only general descriptions have been listed for the fifty-plus breeds. Contact breed clubs or registry associations for specifics. Breed clubs are listed in the back of *Cat Fancy* and *Cats* magazines, and the major registering bodies and a few international clubs are listed below:

# REGISTERING ASSOCIATIONS

*Scottish Fold*

The American Cat Association, Inc. (ACA)
8101 Katherine Avenue
Panorama City, CA 91402
818-762-6080

American Cat Fanciers' Association, Inc. (ACFA)
P.O. Box 203
Point Lookout, MO 65726
417-334-5430

Canadian Cat Association (CCA)
52 Dean Street
Brampton, Ontario
Canada L6W 1M6
416-459-1481

The Cat Fanciers' Association Inc. (CFA)
1805 Atlantic Avenue
P.O. Box 1005
Manasquan, NJ 08736-1005
908-528-9797

Cat Fanciers' Federation (CFF)
9509 Montgomery Road
Cincinnati, OH 45242
513-984-1841

The International Cat Association (TICA)
P.O. Box 2684
Harlingen, TX 78551
512-428-8046

RAS Cat Control of Australia
Ms. Carole Wang
P.O. Box 4317
Sydney NSW 2001
Australia
02- 331-9135

United Cat Federation (UCF)
5510 Ptolemy Way
Mira Loma, CA 91752
714-685-7896

© Norvia Behling

*© Marc Henrie*

LEGEND: When the priest Mun-Ha died, his soul went into his cat Sinh; abruptly, the cat's golden eyes turned blue, hair along his spine became gold, and brown feet blanched white where they touched the holy man. Not only Sinh, but all the temple cats changed, miraculously founding the Sacred Cat of Burma.

## ABYSSINIAN

The Abyssinian looks like a miniature cougar and is known for "agouti" fur. Each hair is "ticked" with two to three bands of color, giving the short, silky coat a wild look. In the United States, Abys are accepted in ruddy, red, and blue. The Abys is a fine-boned, medium-size cat with a lithe and muscular body, and gold-green eyes.

It was once believed Abyssinians resulted from a cross between a cat and a wild rabbit. Abys do not make good lap cats. These intelligent, athletic kitties can jump from the floor to the top of a door with ease. They need (demand!) lots of attention; easily bored, miscreants may be found rifling cupboards or climbing drapes, all with a look of beguiling innocence. To sustain their energy, most Abys have huge appetites. Abys are wonderfully entertaining cats.

*Abyssinian*

## AMERICAN BOBTAIL

This cat is the result of matings between domestic and wild bobcats and has only recently been recognized as a breed. Rose Estes has been breeding Bobtails for fourteen years and calls them intelligent, watchful cats with a sense of mischievousness. "They often sit and plot what's going to be a great joke and then do it," she says.

Males often reach twenty pounds, and the markings may include Siamese points or blue eyes. According to Rose, wild bobcats interbreed most often with Siamese because the scent of the Siamese in season closely resembles the smell of the female bobcat.

As the name implies, Bobtails have abbreviated tails; the gene controlling tail length is missing when the two species breed, resulting in a variety of tail lengths. Standards are still changing, but most Bobtails will have characteristics of both the Siamese and wild bobcats.

# AMERICAN CURL

This kitty's ears curl vertically, away from the head at their outer edges. The Curl is a semi-foreign type, but not cobby, and comes in either short or long fur, and in every color in the rainbow. The American Curl is a mutation discovered in 1981, and breed standards haven't been fully established. Betty Bond, a breeder of Curls, calls them a curious cat. "Curls have more stamina than Scottish Folds and are very playful, without being wired." Curls are whimsical, attractive kitties.

*Right: American Curl*
*Far right: Bengal*

© Marc Henrie

# AMERICAN WIREHAIR

The American Wirehair is the same as an American Shorthair, except with curly fur. A mutant red and white male kitten born in 1966 from a shorthair founded the breed. The guard hairs are crimped and hooked on the end, making the fur frizzy and wiry. The coat feels like a soft, woolly lamb. This is an endearing, versatile cat.

# BALINESE

This long-haired cat developed from a mutation that first appeared in the United States about 1950. The fine, medium-length silky fur lies flat to the body, with no woolly undercoat. The erect tail gracefully waves from side to side as kitty walks, looking like a Balinese dancer. Except for length of coat, the temperament, conformation, and color are the same as the Siamese.

# BENGAL

Bengals are a hybrid cross between the domestic shorthair and the Asian Leopard Cat. About the size of American Shorthairs, they're known for short-to-medium-length, thick, silky fur that's spotted or marbled. The preferred pattern is leopard spots over the body, with ivory to white undersides. Rounded ears are also strived for, and a Bengal's tail must always have a black tip.

Roger Davis breeds these athletic, exotic-looking cats. "Bengals figure things out," he says. "Nothing's sacred in the house, but they do it in such a way you can't get upset with them." A good Bengal will slink when it walks, and the tail carriage is usually low like wild cats. Although Bengals have a wilder-sounding scream than most domestic kitties, they tend to be enthusiastic purrers.

© Richard Katris/Chanan Photography

© Richard Katris/Chanan Photography

## BURMESE

The Burmese has a dark body with discernable darker points. Sable is the most widely accepted color variety. Modern Burmese trace their ancestry to a Siamese hybrid, and today the standard is a medium-size cat of a muscular, modified-foreign body type, with short, satinlike fur. Gold or yellow eyes are preferred.

Burmese like to talk, and have a sassy nature. Burmese thrive on hugs around your neck and, in general, are cats that need a lot of attention.

## BIRMAN

The Birman is a beautiful, long-haired cat marked with dark points like the Himalayan—except the Birman's feet look like they've been dipped in white powdered sugar. Birmans have round heads and full cheeks, a roman nose, and almond-shaped blue eyes. Their bodies aren't cobby like the Persian's, but long and massive, with thick legs and a medium-length plumy tail. The silky coat is easy to groom but needs daily attention. This kitty's personality is somewhere between the placid Persian and extrovert Siamese—an affectionate, inquisitive cat.

## BOMBAY

The Bombay is a black patent leather cat. It was named for its resemblance to the Indian Black Leopard. The breed was created by crossing a Burmese and an American Black Shorthair.

The head is basically round but with a short muzzle; large yellow or copper eyes and medium ears give a distinctly foreign cast. The body is lithe but not thin, with medium-length legs and tail. The Bombay's black fur is short, very glossy, and very thick. Bombays are playful, intelligent, always curious, and want to be in on everything.

© Marc Henrie

*Above: Birman*

*Left: Burmese*

# BURMILLA

The Burmilla developed from an accidental breeding of a Burmese with a chinchilla, resulting in a cat type halfway between a British shorthair and a Burmese. The Burmilla has big green eyes, and a short, dense, silver-tipped coat. It is a playful, gentle cat, and comes in colors of silver or gold ground, with tipped mantel darker along the spine in black, sepia, blue, chocolate, lilac, caramel, beige, red, cream, or apricot. The tail has distinct rings and is tipped in the color of the shading.

# BURMOIRE

The Burmoire was produced by mating Burmilla with Burmese, and it comes in the same colors as the Burmilla. This kitty resembles the Burmese in type and coat texture, but the color pattern is the same as the Oriental Smoke standard—a point pattern with a smoke color. The Burmoire fur looks like rippling silk.

# CALIFORNIA SPANGLE

Paul Casey developed a spotted, wild-looking cat by combining African and Malayan cats with domestics. California Spangle is a shorthaired kitty that comes in silver, bronze, black, white, charcoal, gold, red, blue, and brown, and has darker spots dotting its body. The breed isn't yet acknowledged in all registries, but was recognized by TICA in 1985.

*Chartreux*

© Chanan Photography

# CHARTREUX

The Chartreux is a gorgeous blue kitty. Some think it a very old natural breed developed in France during the Middle Ages by La Grande Chartreuse monastery monks; others believe it a hybrid of French street cats and the British Blue Shorthair.

The Chartreux is a typical European-type cat, with a cobby, massive body, and a lustrous, short coat that is very plush and glossy. It has a very round face with full cheeks, medium-size ears, and copper or golden eyes. The Chartreux is a quiet, gentle kitty that often prefers the company of people and dogs to that of other cats.

# COLORPOINT SHORTHAIR

A Siamese cat in any color except seal, chocolate, blue, or lilac is a colorpoint. Accepted colors include points in lilac cream, tortoiseshell, blue-cream, and lynx (tabby) in every range of colors. Temperament and conformation are the same as the Siamese. (See Siamese)

© Chanan Photography

## HAVANA BROWN

The Havana Brown was produced by crossing a black shorthair with a seal point Siamese. Consequently, Havanas feature many characteristics of the Siamese, but the head is different. Unlike the straight Siamese nose, the Havana Brown has a distinct dip or "stop" at the eyes, and also a definite whisker break. It has short, extremely glossy, chestnut brown fur, and is an active, vocal cat that thrives on attention.

Sheila Ullmann breeds Havanas, and says they're extremely trainable, and can be halter and leash trained. "Havanas are very devoted to any human; even older cats will readily attach to new owners," she says. "They are very oral and enjoy grooming each other. They think it's wonderful to clean their human, too, and will groom your hair at night when you're trying to sleep.

## CYMRIC

The Cymric is a Manx, but with a medium-long, soft, heavy coat. This breed developed from mutant kittens from Manx litters during the 1960s. (See Manx)

## EGYPTIAN MAU

The Egyptian Mau was developed in the United States and is named for the cats worshipped by ancient Egyptian cultures. Its most distinctive feature is mackerel tabby markings that

© Chanan Photography

break to form spots down the back. The Mau is a muscular body Oriental type cat, with a slightly wedge shaped head, green eyes, and big ears. The Mau comes in silver, bronze, smoke, and pewter. This is a very affectionate, somewhat shy cat. It makes an unusual, sweet, chirplike sound.

© Chanan Photography

*Above left: Cymric*

*Below left: Egyptian Mau*

*Left: Havana Brown*

*Above: Himalayan*

*Below: Japanese Bobtail*

© Chanan Photography

## HIMALAYAN

This kitty is a Persian cat with Siamese colorpoint markings. The Himmy is a family cat that has a touch of Siamese curiosity, with the Persian's placid temperament and pleasant, quiet voice. Other than color, the Himalayan conforms to Persian standards.

© Chanan Photography

## JAPANESE BOBTAIL

This "bunny-tailed" kitty was imported to the United States from Japan in the 1970s and can be traced in the Far East back to the seventh century. Its unique tail, which is normally carried erect, has bushy hair fanning to form a pompon. A recessive gene causes the tailbone to twist and curl and the vertebrae to fuse.

This is a slender, medium-size cat; high cheeks and a long parallel nose give unique character to the face. The coat is medium length, without noticeable undercoat, and comes in several colors, the most sought after being black and red patches on a field of white. These cats are not at all timid; they are active (but not hyper), eat ravenously, have sunny dispositions, and are extremely vocal. The Japanese Bobtail is a curious cat that likes to explore the world.

## JAVANESE

The Javanese could be described as a long-haired colorpoint. Liz Layton, a breeder of these exceptional kitties, describes them as being one of the best children's cats she's ever seen. "Javanese are very trainable cats. My cat Akai will come, sit, and stay on request." Liz's other cats often learn just by watching older kitties. "Javanese are also great shoulder cats," says Liz. "If you have more than one, they'll compete for the shoulders!"

## KORAT

The Korat originated in Thailand and is one of the oldest natural breeds. Considered a bringer of luck, the Korat is one of the four major blue breeds and is somewhat rare. The body is cobby; fur is short and plush, with silver-tipped blue hair. In Thailand, it is known as the Si-Sawat, and a true Korat must be able to trace lineage to Thailand. Korats are mild-mannered, intelligent, and affectionate and not terribly vocal.

© Chanan Photography

## MAINE COON

Maine coons are the oldest American breed. Considered "gentle giants," these cats probably developed from crossing American Shorthair with Angora. They are a substantial cat with stout legs, a round head, and large round eyes. The coat is hard, silky guard hair with no undercoat and needs regular grooming. These kitties are mature by age four to five years.

Tony Kalish, a breeder for twelve years says, "The average weight is eighteen to twenty pounds for males, and ten to fifteen pounds for females—not the thirty-plus pounds often reported. Coons feel heavier because they have such muscular bodies."

These active cats need space to exercise. They enjoy playing with water and will get right in the tub with you. "They're extremely gregarious," says Tony, "and have no sense of propriety. They never grow up; no matter their age, they have a childlike quality."

*Above: Maine Coon*

*Left: Korat*

*Maine Coon*

GALLERY OF BREEDS

## MALAYAN

The Malayan is a Burmese cat, but comes instead in colors of champagne, platinum, and blue.

## MANX

© Chanan Photography

Legend says the Manx lost its tail when Noah closed the Ark door too soon and cut it off. The tailless Manx developed on the Isle of Man about the sixteenth century. He looks like a British Shorthair, but longer rear legs give him a raised rear end, like a race car. The mutant gene responsible for taillessness results in only a small hollow where a tail would be; some Manx have residual tails, known as risers, stumpies or stubbies, and longies, according to length of tail. Manx come in all colors except chocolate, lavender, or point pattern.

Manx breeder Elaine Dunham characterizes this cat as full of fun. "They're very playful and loving, and can jump straight up off the ground, as if on springs." The Manx is a "people cat" that loves to cuddle on laps.

*Above: Norwegian Forest*

*Below: Ocicat*

*Opposite page: Manx*

## NORWEGIAN FOREST CAT

Written descriptions make the "Wegie" sound like a Maine coon, except the Norwegian head is shorter and more triangular, and the double coat is thicker. Also called the Skogkatt, the breed is probably much older than the Maine coon; Norse legend describes just such a mysterious, enchanted animal. Any color is permitted.

Lynne Boroff breeds these magnificent kitties and describes them as very outgoing, almost puppylike in behavior. "They'll come to the door to greet you when you come home. They're very athletic and are great climbers; they can jump straight up like a yo-yo." Wegies demand attention but are very quiet and don't meow all day long.

## OCICAT

© Chanan Photography

When breeders tried to produce an Aby-pointed Siamese, they got a spotted cat with a tabby face that looks like a small ocelot. The hybrid body type looks superficially like a Mau, but the head shape is less foreign. This active kitty is quite large, and very well muscled. The large almond eyes are slightly slanted and can be any color but blue. The coat color comes in twelve varieties, including cinnamon, chocolate, tawny, fawn, lavender, and varieties of silver. Breeder Barbara Love says Ocicats are very affectionate, love people, and get along well with other cats and dogs.

GALLERY OF BREEDS
115

© Chanan Photography

## PERSIAN

Persians were the first long-haired cats to reach Europe, sometime in the late 1500s. The Persian is medium to large with a cobby body and short thick legs; the head is round and broad; the ears are small and set far apart. The nose is short with a definite stop; the "peke-faced Persian" nose is nearly a minus! Cheeks are full and eyes large and round without any slant. Long, flowing hair and woolly undercoat come in a variety of colors and patterns. In the United Kingdom, Persians are divided into different Persian breeds according to each color variety (such as black Persians, shaded cameo, etc.).

This is a quiet, docile breed that takes a bit of grooming. "Persians love to lay on the couch and be looked at, almost like they know they're a beautiful cat," notes breeder Mary Jane Riggs. Although they can play, Persians do more sleeping and looking pretty than some cats.

*Above: Red Persian*

*Below: Ragdoll*

*Opposite page: Devon Rex*

© Marc Henrie

## RAGDOLL

The Ragdoll was named for its ability to go limp when handled and looks like a mismarked Birman. This large blue-eyed cat has a round head, a straight nose, and a medium-length coat of silky texture. The Ragdoll comes with or without white mittens, in bicolor, and can have point colors like the Himalayan. This kitty is very placid with a gentle nature.

# REX
# (CORNISH AND DEVON)

Rex cats are named for the Rex rabbit, which also has curly hair. The genetic mutation that makes the hair curl allows only one type of hair instead of the three (awn, down, and guard) that most cats have. Rex cats come in every color, bicolors predominate, and coats should be short, curly, wavy, or rippled.

The Cornish Rex has short, soft, curly fur; even the whiskers are curly. The Cornish Rex is Oriental in appearance with a muscular, small- to medium-size body, and a long, slender torso. The back is naturally arched, and the tail is long and slender. The Devon type is another curly-coated mutation that is a more pixieish cat with fine, wavy soft fur. Both types have muted voices.

Rex breeds shed less than others, and body temperature is about a degree higher than in other cats. These kitties are exceptional jumpers and sprinters. They want to be included and will try to help with everything you do, using their paws like hands to open cupboards and doors. Rexes enjoy being lap cats and love shoulders. Their kittens are precocious and develop earlier than other breeds.

# RUSSIAN BLUE

Russian Blues are thought to have come from Archangel, Russia. This is a foreign-type cat known for its short double-coated, blue fur tipped with silver, which is so plush it can be stroked both ways without exposing the blue skin. The eyes must be vivid green.

The Russian Blue is a quiet, loving cat that craves human company but is not as demanding as some breeds.

© Marc Henrie

# SCOTTISH FOLD/HIGHLAND LOPS

This breed sprang from a genetic abnormality in a kitten born in Scotland in 1961 with flopped ears that folded forward. The body type is similar to the American Shorthair cat and comes in the same colors. Ears should be as small as possible, and the tail rarely reaches full size.

Betty Bond describes her Scottish Folds' personalities as being almost Persian-like, but not quite as laid back. "They're a little more playful, but totally relaxed, and adjust their personality to whatever they're around." Currently only accepted in short coat, long-coated Scottish Folds are called "Highland Lops".

*British Shorthair*

# SHORTHAIRS

Shorthaired cats fall into four types: British, American, Oriental or Foreign, and Exotic. The British is sturdy with a strong, muscular body on short legs, a broad round head, a short straight nose, and big round eyes. The forebears of the British Shorthair probably arrived in Great Britain nearly two thousand years ago. The British Blue Shorthair and British Black Shorthair are two of this variety, designated as separate breeds in the United Kingdom. The American is larger and leaner than the British type, with longer legs, an oblong head, square muzzle with very full cheeks, and a medium-length nose. In both types, color and character are as varied as the rainbow.

The Foreign or Oriental type has a wedge-shaped head with slanting eyes and large, pointed ears, a lithe body with long legs, and a very fine coat. Breeder of Radiance Orientals, Vicki Harrison calls them "Siamese cats in designer jeans." Oriental shorthairs come in all colors not accepted as either Siamese or colorpoint shorthairs.

Exotic shorthairs resulted from interbreeding Persians, American shorthairs, and Burmese. These look like shorthaired, plush-coated Persians. Both color and character span the spectrum.

© Marc Henrie

# SIAMESE

LEGEND: Crossed eyes arose after a Siamese cat stared so hard and long at Buddha's gold goblet, her eyes went funny. Another legend says the Siamese had a knot tied in her tail to remember something—which she hasn't yet remembered. Today, crossed eyes and kinked tails are considered faults.

The Siamese is one of the most popular breeds of cat and has been delighting Westerners for over one hundred years. Siamese have an Oriental body type and upward-sloping, almond-shaped blue eyes. The fur is short and fine and lays flat. Fur body color is cream; the points may be seal, blue, chocolate, or lilac.

The darker markings are related to heat: the cooler the body temperature, the darker the fur. In very cold climates, a Siamese may be entirely dark! Siamese are opinionated, loyal cats that are outgoing, intelligent, very trainable, playful, and exceptionally vocal. Siamese talk back to you, even when you've not spoken. They are, in short, wonderful companions.

Controversy exists between factions trying to establish breed standards and origins. A Siberia Cat belonging to breeder David Boehm gave birth October 1990 to the first Siberia Cats born in America. "These cats are more affectionate and devoted than Norwegian or Maine Coon cats," he says, but warns, "Don't play rough with them, or they'll play rough back."

*Siamese kitten*

# SIBERIA CAT

The breed was accepted by Russian Cat Fancy only three years ago and was first imported to the United States in 1990. This large, rugged, long-haired cat is reminiscent of the Maine coon and Norwegian forest cat. According to provisional standards set by TICA, Siberias have a modified wedge-shaped head with large, almost oval eyes, and medium low-set ears. The coat is of medium length with lustrous, oily guard hairs and minimal undercoat. Females weigh thirteen to seventeen pounds, males seventeen to twenty-six pounds.

# SINGAPURA

Once known as the Drain Cat for its habit of seeking shelter there, the Singapura is native to Singapore. This is a medium- to small-size cat of a foreign type. The ticked coat is like an Abyssinian but has a smoother satiny feel. Brown is the only color currently accepted. Mary Jane Riggs says her Singapur "Ada" likes to squirrel things away. "She's into stuff all the time; you'll have a pencil on the table, and the next thing you know it'll be in the bathroom behind the toilet." Singapuras are playful, active cats that love to climb and perch on shoulders.

THE INCOMPARABLE CAT

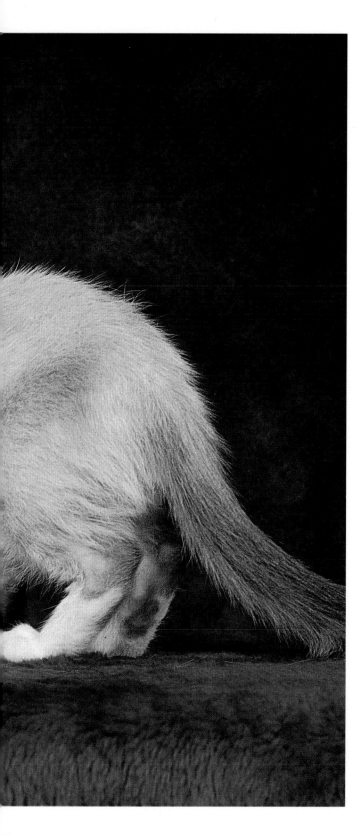

## SNOWSHOE

This kitty looks like a Siamese but has the Birman's white feet. The Siamese body type is slightly larger and heavier in the Snowshoe. This beautiful cat also has an outgoing personality.

## SOMALI

The Somali looks like a little fox and is actually an Abyssinian with long fur. Adult coats are full, silky, and easy to groom, but take about eighteen months to develop from dark kitten color to full ticking. Somalis are friendly and athletic, and they often use paws like little monkeys, poking and getting into everything. If you like the Aby but prefer long fur, this is the cat for you.

*Left: Snowshoe*

*Below:  Somali*

© Marc Henrie

# SPHYNX

This unusual-looking, hairless cat developed in 1966 from a mutant kitten born in Ontario, Canada. The Sphynx is not entirely hairless, but has fine "peach fuzz" and small amounts of hair on the points. Because it lacks hair, this kitty can't cope with extremes in temperature and may suffer from sunburn. The Sphynx comes in any coat color.

Sphynx breeder Pat Depew says, "If you sit down, they're right in your lap and come running to you like a little puppy." Sphynx are extremely friendly and act like no one is a stranger. They will go from person to person in a crowd.

*Right: Sphynx*

*Far right: Tonkinese*

# SPOTTED MIST

The Spotted Mist breed was first developed in Australia by crossing a Burmese and Abyssinian with a domestic tabby. This is a medium-size foreign type, known for its delicate spots against a misty ground color. The legs and tail are ringed, and the face is lined like other tabby varieties. This very affectionate kitty comes in the same range of colors as Burmese.

# TIFFANY

The Tiffany was produced by crossing Burmese with Persians, and is the same as a Burmese in type and coloring, but with long hair. If you liked the Burmese but want silky fur and a plumy tail, this is the cat for you.

# TONKINESE

The Tonkinese, also called the "Golden Siamese," is a result of a Siamese and Burmese cross. Visually, the Tonkinese is somewhere between the two. This foreign type cat's head lacks the straight lines of the Siamese, and the Tonkinese's cheeks are more full and rounded. They come in the same point colors as Siamese, with the darker body color of the Burmese, and eyes should be blue-green or turquoise.

Breeder Elaine Dunham says the Tonkinese and Burmese have similar personalities. Tonkinese are vocal like a Siamese but less strident. "Tonkinese are like precocious and curious children. Never underestimate them—they refuse to be bored." She suggests establishing rules early, because these are intelligent cats that will outsmart you given half an inch.

## TURKISH ANGORA

The elegant Angora is a very old breed from which Persians were created. The head is not at all like the Persians, and should be wedge-shaped, with a straight nose and almond eyes slanting slightly toward the nose. The body is long and elegant, and the bone structure is dainty compared to cobby Persians. Fur is very fine and silky, with just a hint of curling on longer hairs, but should lay flat to the body, without any woolly undercoat. The coat needs regular grooming to stay in shape. The traditional color is pure white, but the breed is now accepted in any color recognized in foreign shorthairs. This kitty is docile, graceful, and very affectionate. It enjoys playing but isn't as boisterous as a Siamese.

## TURKISH VAN

The Turkish Van, or Turkish Swimming Cat, comes from the Lake Van area in southeast Turkey and has been domesticated for several hundred years. This cat is similar to the Angora. The Van is a striking white cat with auburn markings on the tail, ears, and cap of the head between the ears or eyes. The Van has the same pleasant nature as the Angora and loves the water.

Karen Hooker says her Vans never tire of playing fetch. "I wake up in the morning with little paper balls on my head where they've dropped them trying to wake me up to play." Vans are very loyal, not at all subtle, and can figure out how to get into anything.

## CONCLUSION

*The Cat Companion* has been a delight to prepare. I hope you'll share the tips and tricks, facts and fables found in these pages to introduce others to the joy of being cat-owned.

It was my intention to answer many questions, but I also wanted to whet your appetite for more. Learning about *Felis silvestris catus* is an ongoing adventure for us all, and educating ourselves can only help us be better caretakers for these mischievous, alluring creatures we call cats.

Kitty has traveled thousands of miles and hundreds of centuries to snuggle in our laps today. Responsible cat lovers like you will ensure that she continues to hold a special place as a valued companion and pampered pet in the hearts of future generations.

Whisker twitches and kitty kisses; kneading paws and fluffy purrs; damp noses and velvet cheeks; tongue tickles and shoulder perches. A small, warm fur-child winds about your ankles, sending her message in unmistakable felinese. No matter how she shows it, the action speaks louder than words; warm, furry, unconditional LOVE.

Oh beautiful, mysterious Cat, the feeling is so mutual!

*Turkish Van*

© Marc Henrie

Beadle, Muriel. *The Cat: History, Biology and Behavior.* New York: Simon and Schuster, 1977.

Brown, Beth, compiled by. *The Wonderful World of Cats.* New York: Harper and Brothers, 1961.

Chandoha, Walter, collected by. *The Literary Cat.* Philadelphia: Lippincott Company, 1977

Eckstein, Warren, and Fay. *How To Get Your Cat To Do What You Want.* New York: Villard Books, 1990.

Fox, Dr. Michael W. *Understanding Your Cat.* New York: Coward, McCann and Geoghegan, Inc., 1974.

Gallico, Paul W. *The Silent Miaow.* New York: Crown Publishers, Inc., 1964.

Gettings, Fred. *Ghosts in Photographs.* New York: Harmony Books, 1978.

Gettings, Fred. *The Secret Lore of the Cat.* New York: Carol Publishing Group, 1989.

Holland, Barbara. *Secrets of the Cat: Its Lore, Legend, and Lives.* New York: Ballantine Books, 1988.

Howey, M. Oldfield. *The Cat in the Mysteries of Religion and Magic.* Secaucus, New Jersey: Castle Books, 1956.

Johnson, Pam. *Cat Love: Understanding the Needs and Nature of Your Cat.* Pownal, Vermont: Storey Communications, Inc., 1990.

Jones, Jill-Marie, ed. *Pet Health News Magazine.* 3 Burroughs, Irvine, CA 92718: Fancy Publications, Inc.

Lampe, Dr. Kenneth F., and McCann, Mary Ann. *AMA Handbook of Poisonous and Injurious Plants.* Chicago: Copr. American Medical Association, 1985.

Lewis, Gogo, and Manley, Sean, selected by. *Cat Encounter's: A Cat Lover's Anthology.* New York: Lothrop, Lee & Shepard Books, 1979.

Loxton, Howard. *The Noble Cat.* Published by Portland House. Distributed by New York: Random House, 1990.

Morris, Desmond. *Cat Lore.* New York: Crown Publishers, Inc., 1987.

Muncaster, Alice L., and Sawyer, Ellen. *The Black Cat Make Me Buy It!* New York: Crown Publishers, Inc., 1988.

Muncaster, Alice L., and Yanow, Ellen. *The Cat Made Me Buy It!* New York: Crown Publishers, Inc., 1984.

Muncaster, Alice L., and Sawyer, Ellen Yanow. *The Cat Sold It!* New York: Crown Publishers, Inc., 1986.

O'Neil, John P. *Metropolitan Cats.* New York: Harry N. Abrams, Inc., Publishers, 1981.

Praded, Joni, director and ed. *Animals Magazine.* 13505 Huntington Ave., Boston, MA 02130: Massachusetts Society for the Prevention of Cruelty to Animals.

Segnor, K.E. *Cat Fancy.* 3 Burroughs, Irvine, CA 92718: Fancy Publications, Inc.

Taylor, David. *The Ultimate Cat Book.* New York: Simon and Schuster, 1989.

Torregrossa, Adriano. *Color Treasury of Cats and Kittens.* Novara: Instituo Geografico de Agnostini, 1967.

Walton, Linda J., ed. *Cats Magazine.* 445 Merrimac Dr., Port Orange, FL 32127: Cats Magazine Inc.

Boehm, David, ed. *The 1990 Guinness Book of World Records.* Sterling Publishing Co., Inc, 1990.

# INDEX